FINDING MY SHOES

My Journey of Overcoming 10 Years of
Homelessness and Addiction to
Becoming One of America's Most
Sought After Educators and
Motivational Speakers

Dr. Brenda Combs, Ed.D.
Ambassador of Inspiration

Finding My Shoes

My Journey of Overcoming 10 Years of Homelessness and Addiction to Becoming One of America's Most Sought After Educators and Motivational Speakers

ISBN- 978-0692557716

BRC Publishing

BrendaCombs.com

Printed in the United States

Norma

Never give up!

Brenda Combs

Dedication

This book is dedicated to anyone who is dealing with life issues and struggles. I hope that my story will inspire you to believe in yourself. You already have what it takes to be successful and make your goals and dreams reality. It all starts with believing in yourself. You must tell yourself that you are intelligent and capable of achieving greatness. Make it a priority to make the right choice and do the right thing even when no one is watching.

Brenda

Acknowledgments

Tony, you have always been by my side for better or for worse. You believe in me and push me to be better. Quentin and Laura, you are the best team a girl could ever hope for. I am so blessed for your faith in me.

My parents (Payton & Carrie Mae Combs; Walter & Hazel Bell), and siblings, Dwight, Sharon, LaFronce (Jackie) Pamela, Clarence, thank you for accepting me for who I am.

To all my Uncles, Aunts, Grandparents, cousins, and Bill "Pops", Jordan, Mama Penny Priest, I love you to life! Family is everything to me.

My sistahs (Patti, Beth, Terrie, Sue, Kathy & Bonita) I am grateful for your love, support, and encouragement.

And finally to Mycole, you are the love of my life and my reason for breathing. You are my total inspiration.

Table Of Contents

Prologue

The summer sun in Arizona is brutal, even in the early daytime hours. Its searing heat was the first thing I noticed when I awoke. Although I had no idea what time it was I guessed it was the middle of the afternoon and my skin was already burning, my mouth was dry, my tongue swollen, and my lips were cracked and stinging. Then I noticed my head was throbbing and my stomach churning.

I was lying on a discarded sofa in the alley. Although I was familiar with most of the alleys in this part of downtown Phoenix, it took a while for me to figure out exactly where I was. I had no memory of how I got here.

I tried to sit up, but the slightest movement sent convulsions of pain through my entire body. I felt as though I had been beaten. I wanted to lie back down and sleep, but I had already been in the sun too long and I was overcome with a great thirst, my mouth so dry that I couldn't swallow.

I felt dizzy, weak. As I tried to reconstruct the events of the previous day, slowly I began to remember. Several images floated through my mind – going with some friends to party, smoking crack, drinking, taking a pill that I thought was Demerol and passing out, waking up in an unfamiliar room with a stranger pinning me to the floor with his body. As those images came into sharper focus, I felt my stomach turn. A rush of nausea swept through me. Even though I had just slept for several hours, I was bone-tired, exhausted. It was all I could do to roll over to avoid vomiting on myself.

I turned and vomited – and that's when I saw the cat with orange fur lying in the dirt beside the sofa. She hadn't even flinched when I made my commotion. She was dead. She must have come here to rest for the night, like I did. Poor thing. Looking at that cat I saw myself. I just wandered away from home one day. I lost my bearings and lost my way. I lost everything until there was just one last thing to lose.

That's how I got here, to this alley off Garfield street, located smack in the middle of what is known by the Phoenix Police Department as "The Zone." It is one of those places that everybody has pretty much given up on, including the cops, the city officials and,

most of all, the people whose misfortune it is to call this section of Phoenix home.

The houses, mostly built in the 1950s and 1960s, are small and cramped, boxes of cinder block and brick slathered over with peeling stucco. Here and there are hints of landscaping, which suggest that once, long, long ago, the people who lived in these houses had at least made an effort, that they had exhibited some semblance of pride in their neighborhood.

A scattering of majestic palm trees shoot up in haughty defiance amidst the decay, but for the most part what landscaping has endured, has grown wild and deformed from decades of indifference. Long-neglected roses still offer their blooms, but rather than dispel the grim surroundings, their petals stand out in hideous relief and looking at them you realize that sometimes there is nothing more painful than a reminder of how things used to be.

The small lawns are strewn with junk and garbage, the sort of place where wild-blown trash collects against wobbly chain-link fences. A few patches of grass stubbornly cling to the baked earth, but most of the lawns yield crops of only dust and weeds. The yards, alleys and curbs are strewn with broken beer bottles, discarded hypodermic needles and waste, both animal and human. Each summer evening, the wind blows and a yellow-brown blanket of dust settles over The Zone like a stained sheet covering a derelict.

Many of the houses are boarded up, having been abandoned by their owners. But that is not to say they are unoccupied. They are crack houses now. But the truth is, just about every house in The Zone is a crack house, abandoned or not.

If there were ever a concentrated effort to fight drugs in this neighborhood, the cause has long since been abandoned. Nobody complains now. It is a neighborhood filled with drug dealers, prostitutes, petty criminals, and drug users.

Maybe the cops just figure leaving the dealer and addicts alone rather than dispersing them that there's certain logic to that. This is a place where hopelessness has been quarantined.

A handful of elderly people live here, too. They moved into the neighborhood back in the foggy past, when people made an effort to

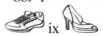

live like humans. Now, they are trapped here and, if they are lucky, they simply don't notice anymore the squalor that engulfs their little neighborhood.

So, no, I don't imagine anybody here paid any attention to the cat. Why would they? Not here. Not in the part of the city where prostitutes perform their acts in broad daylight and plain view. Not in the part of the city where the flickering glow of a hundred crack pipes lights the night skies like a great swarm of fireflies in a country meadow. Not in the part of the city where people exist on instinct, impulse, and animal drive.

Nobody would notice a cat in a place like this.

Still, I can't help but wonder about that cat now and then. I wonder where she came from and what her life must have been before she arrived in this alley. She probably is just one of the thousands of feral cats that are common to large urban areas. But I prefer to imagine her as a family pet that wandered off one day and never found her way back home.

I like to imagine that she was once loved, that she had a place in this world, and that she mattered.

I guess I like to think of her that way because we have a lot in common, me and that cat. On a June day in 1995, we shared this alley for a few desperate hours. By then, life for both of us had degenerated into a pathetic, pointless struggle. We had been abused and neglected, degraded and forgotten. We staggered blindly on, trying to sustain a life that hardly seemed worth the effort.

The cat died. I lived. My name is Dr. Brenda Combs. Welcome to my story.

x

Part I

Chapter 1
"Homeless at Home"

Those who had met me at my worst - in the late 80's to mid-1990s – probably saw me as not much more than a drug addict who relied on crime and guile to support her crack cocaine habit. They might have assumed that I had been raised in poverty, perhaps by a single mom in a community rife with violence and drug abuse. They might have assumed I had dropped out of school early and never held a regular job. That I grew up never feeling loved, nurtured, or safe.

Those assumptions would have been pretty accurate when applied to most of the people I met during my time on the streets of Phoenix.

But that wasn't my experience.

I grew up in a good home, with two loving attentive parents who sacrificed to provide a safe and stable childhood.

And yet, somehow I never felt I belonged. I cannot really point to any specific reason that I would feel strangely disconnected from that loving family, which included my parents and a younger sister and brother. Yet even as a small child, surrounded by my parents and siblings, I felt as though I was somehow on the periphery of the family.

I wonder sometimes if it is possible to be born with amnesia. It seems like most of my life has been a struggle to find out who I am. If you don't know who you are, you can't know where you belong. And to me, the definition of home is

a place where you feel you belong. And in that case, I think I've been homeless most of my life.

I was born on August 23, 1962 in Bentonia, Mississippi and my parents, who never married, went their separate ways soon after I was born. When I was about two years old, my mother moved to Flagstaff, Arizona – she had an aunt who lived there. My biological dad moved to Los Angeles at roughly the same time.

Soon after the move, my mother married a man, the father who legally adopted me when I was five. Although my biological father is in my life today and a big part of my family, my Daddy Payton Combs has always been my daddy. I think God knew I was going to be a handful which is why I have two sets of parents!

Our family soon included not only my mother and me, but my brother Dwight, and my sister Sharon. Dwight is three years younger than me; Sharon is four years my junior. Our daddy worked extremely hard to provide for all of us. He had no more than a high school diploma, but he had a great work ethic. Most of my school years he worked two jobs.

Flagstaff had a population of about 30,000 when I was a child there. The town was built on tourism – it is the place you stay when visiting the Grand Canyon or ski at Snow Bowl – and education. Flagstaff is home to Northern Arizona University (NAU).

During the day, my dad worked at the dining hall on campus. At night, he would clean office buildings downtown. Although he had little time during the week, he was an attentive father, who devoted his weekends to us. My mom worked as a cook at a restaurant just a few blocks from campus. Although the pay wasn't great, the hours were a perfect fit for a working mom. She worked from 8 a.m. until 2 p.m., which meant she was there to get her children off to school in the morning and back home before we arrived home from school.

Most weekdays my brother, sister, and I would come home after school let out, eat a snack, and do our homework. Sometimes after we finished our schoolwork, my mother would sing with us. I loved these times. Mom put all her heart and soul into her singing. "Amazing Grace" was her favorite composition. Her powerful voice was alto soprano, a cross between Aretha Franklin and Shirley Caesar, was so laden with emotion, it never failed to send chills down my spine.

Weekends were devoted to family. Because ours was a very spiritual household, much of my social life revolved around church. My mother sang in the church choir and my dad served as a deacon and church treasurer. I grew up singing in church, too.

When I was 5, my mother decided to learn piano. Each week, her piano teacher would help my mom as she tried to master "What a Friend We Have in Jesus." My mother would practice playing the tune over and over. But each time she would arrive at one part of the tune and mess up. Over and over, she would move through the tune and then hit the troublesome passage and fail miserably.

One day as she struggled through the tune and failed yet again at the critical moment, she turned to her teacher and said, exasperated, "Let's go have some tea."

As the women went into kitchen, I climbed up on the piano stool and began to play "What a Friend We Have in Jesus." It was a flawless performance. When I finished, I looked up to see my mom and the piano teacher standing in the doorway. They had tears in their eyes.

When I was just a little girl, my favorite TV shows were "American Bandstand" and "Soul Train" and Saturday mornings would find me sitting in the front of the TV transfixed, imaging myself as one of the teens dancing and singing on the shows. I was especially fond of "Soul Train." After the show was over, like most young girls, I would retreat to my bedroom where I would practice my dance moves and sing into my "microphone," which was a hairbrush.

Soon, I began picking out the tunes I had heard on "Bandstand" or "Soul Train," by ear on our piano. When I was about eight years old, I began playing the piano during church services. My mom, a deeply spiritual woman, was especially proud of me when I played the piano at church and she encouraged me, paying for piano lessons so that I could learn to read music. Although leaning to read and play music was often drudgery for a young girl, insisting on lessons was one of the best gifts my mom ever gave me. (Thank you Mama).

My parents bought a little house in the predominantly ethnic south Flagstaff for $6,000 in 1966. They worked hard, saved money and, about 10 years later, moved into a nicer home in a nicer area of town. It's the typical American dream, I guess. They devoted their lives to building a better life for their family. They lived conservatively and dreamed, conservatively, too.

They didn't smoke, drink, go out dancing, or even out together as a couple for date night. Everything was about working, paying the bills, and taking care of the children. Their dream for each one of us was for their children to have a good education, and when we grew up, to hold a job with benefits, own a car, and a house.

Now that I am a parent, I can appreciate the challenge that all parents face in raising children. Parents want to provide a safe, happy home for our children. And most of all, we want to protect them from influences that will cause them harm.

My parents were no different.

Let me be clear on one important point: I do not blame my parents for the horrible course my life would take. But I do sometimes wonder if my life might have turned out differently if a few things in my childhood had been different.

I didn't grow up in an abusive home, nor was our home unhappy. But my parents did have some very definite views on child-rearing and the rules they established from my perspective served to alienate me from my peers. They were extremely overly protective. I understand it now, but not back then.

Sleepovers were not allowed. When my friend Mimi from NAU invited me to her birthday slumber party, my mother said no. "The seldom you visit, the better friends you'll be," she told me. I never once spent the night at a friend's house during my childhood.

In junior high my friends Viola, Liz, and Christine invited me over to their houses after school, but I was not allowed to go.

I was not allowed to date as a teen. I could attend school dances, but was required to leave by 10 p.m., about the time the dances were really getting started.

Just about anything we did outside of the home we did in the company of family. I never really got to know many of my classmates outside the narrow confines of school.

Young girls, I am convinced, learn about themselves through their friendships. But when I look back on my childhood, I realize that I never developed the type of close friendships most girls dream about. I had friends but I also had trust issues even back then so I never had that close friend with whom you can share your deepest fears, insecurities and dreams.

Without those friendships, I withdrew into myself. With no one to confide in, I soon began to feel that the self-doubts and insecurities that a young girl feels were unique to me. Left alone with those fears, I began to develop a poor self-image.

I would listen to the other girls talk about the places they went, things they had done, the sleep-overs and dates and house parties and I realize that I had nothing to share. What's more, the girls seemed to have an air of confidence about them. Going to parties and dances enabled those girls to be comfortable around boys in social settings. Me? I was painfully shy and awkward around boys, so I didn't get much attention from them. At least not from my point of view.

It was the close, best-friend relationship that I most desperately wanted, though. Let me be clear I had friends. Friends to hang out with at lunch, in between classes, school dances, and I was grateful and appreciative of them in my life. I also had casual friendships. These never developed any real close bonds. I found that it was much easier to stay to myself. I felt ugly and strange and unlikable. I was different. I hated being different. Most kids do.

When I turned 16, I was able to convince my parents to let me have a birthday party. To me, the party represented a chance to really connect with my peers socially. Our family had just moved from the south side to the north side of town. House parties were what my friends were used to. So when we planned it, I asked my parents if we could have a cake, some chips, and some punch. My parents' notion of a party turned out to be as sharp contrast to what I had envisioned. Essentially, the party they planned would be the sort you would throw for a 12-year-old.

Early on, I remember one of the girls plopping on the sofa and muttering, "This is so boring!"

Everyone made some excuse to leave early. I was crushed. I was humiliated and embarrassed. I went to bed early and cried myself to sleep.

I'm certain my parents didn't impose these rules out of cruelty. I think, for them, the rules – rigid though they might be – were intended to shelter their children from the dangers they saw all around them. In our neighborhood, you didn't have to look far to find teens that were using drugs or getting pregnant or committing crimes.

My parents were determined to protect their children from those dangers. Now that I am a parent, I can appreciate those fears.

But in my case, at least, their efforts to shelter me served also to isolate me. I also think that, to a large degree, the problem was a matter of personality.

From my earliest memories, I was always the one in the family who loved adventures, who loved to try new things. That curiosity, I think, was a natural byproduct of my creative nature. Dwight and Sharon, much like my parents, seemed to find comfort in the familiar. But for me, the rules were a prison, keeping me away from everything new and exciting. Now I will say that I had a great relationship with my cousins. They were more like brothers and sisters. We had some amazing times growing up. I was also very blessed to have the opportunity to spend time with all of my grandparents. Summer vacations were so much fun when we would drive to Texas, Louisiana, and Mississippi to visit family. This part of my life is filled with happy memories that have lasted a lifetime! This is probably why family is everything to me.

My parents never really understood that. To them, my desire to explore the world outside the narrow confines of home, family and church were the mark of a rebellious spirit. My parents preached humility, church, and family. But I wanted to be in the spotlight. To them, that represented a lack of humility, a flaw in my character that could only be corrected through strict adherence to uncompromising rules.

When I was 12, my mom told me that about my biological father. She told me my biological father was a man named Walter Bell, who was now living in Los Angeles with his wife, Hazel.

Over the next couple of years, I reconnected with Walter and his family, which by then included two half-sisters, Jackie and Pam.

The more I learned about Walter and his family, the more intrigued I became. Walter and Hazel unlike my parents, whose lives revolved around family and a small circle of friends, traveled in much larger circles. They worked hard, and raised their family, but they also went places, socialized, smoked cigarettes, drank, and had house parties. Compared to my very conservative parents, Walter and Hazel lived exciting lives, constantly being exposed to new people and new experiences in a big city.

When I was 14, I ran away from home. My plan was to go live with Walter and Hazel in L.A., the city that had Hollywood, concerts, comedy shows, fashion, and celebrities. How much more interesting it would be than Flagstaff, with its one roller rink, movie theater, and modest mall. I thought I was being so clever the day I snuck out of the house bright and early, headed to the Greyhound bus depot, bought a ticket, and headed for L.A. I made it as far as Phoenix before I got caught.

I realized that if I couldn't physically escape, I could escape in another way. More and more, I retreated into my own fantasy world.

When I was a sophomore, I stumbled across a book called *Two Girls from New York*. It was the tale of two teenage girls living in a world of glamour and glitz. I must have read that book twenty times or more. Before long, I began to see myself as one of the characters in the story, living in a big city and pursuing my dreams. I saw myself in limousines and fancy clothes and fine restaurants. In my fantasy, my name was up in lights and people wanted to know me, and to be my friend. How different that would be from my real life.

"Stop dreaming," my mother said to me over and over each time I voiced my hopes of one day singing on Broadway or even on TV, maybe even living in New York City or L.A. I can remember her telling me over and over again while she was driving the three of us in the car, or during the times the whole family was sitting at the kitchen table, or as she and I worked in the garden together. "Stay in school and get an education, so you can find a good job with benefits." Both of my parents were practical people.

After a while, I learned not to share my dreams.

Chapter 2
"An Odd Shade of Black"

Race has never been a big deal or issue to me.

I realize that on some level this may sound self-serving. Most people would love to believe that they are color-blind on this issue, of course.

When Martin Luther King Jr. expressed his dream of a world where a person is judged "not by the color of his skin, but by the content of his character," the words spoke to the hearts of decent people of all races. There are, after all, few people who will openly admit that race plays a significant role in how they view people.

To be perfectly honest, my views on race aren't so much a reflection of my morals or character as they are a function of my somewhat unique experiences.

I've come to believe that prejudices thrive on unfamiliarity; a child most often does not like a food because he has tried it, but because he has not.

I am convinced that segregation, whether it is the legally-imposed type of the pre-Civil Rights era, self-imposed or socio-economic, is an enormous obstacle to harmony. I was able to escape that isolation at an early age and I can't help but believe that the exposure I gained from those years, although sometimes painful, did much to shape my attitude toward race. If my experiences had been different, it's reasonable to assume that my views would reflect that, too.

23

What I do know is that I interacted with white people far more than most of the other black kids in my neighborhood by virtue of going to elementary school at the predominantly white Northern Arizona University Elementary School. For my parents, the decision was mostly practical; they both worked near the university.

I attended NAU Elementary School through the fifth grade. It was there that I first learned how to interact with people of a different racial background. It was also there that I first experienced the bitter reality of racism and discrimination.

Young children are not generally inclined to have strong convictions about race. It is almost always a learned behavior. More often than not, children are curious about things that are different, so my presence at NAU Elementary was not initially a traumatizing experience.

But that began to change as I progressed through elementary school. My first exposure to racism came in the second or third grade when I found myself in class with a kid named Grover.

Grover was an angry kid from my perspective. And for whatever reason, he took a strong disliking to me. We saw each other around school. I generally tried to avoid him. The first time he had the opportunity to talk to me he walked right up and said, "You're a nigger."

This was a new word to me. I had no idea what it meant, but I was pretty sure it wasn't a compliment. It seemed to me that Grover was accusing me of something.

When I got home from school that day, Mom was in our kitchen, cooking dinner. I looked at the pictures of Martin Luther King, Jr. and President John F. Kennedy hanging up on the walls.

"Mom?" I asked. "What's a nigger?"

Mom was at the sink, with her back to me, but I could see her stiffen. She seemed to be trying to compose herself. It took her a few moments.

She turned to face me, dish-rag in hand.

"Where did you hear that word?" she asked in a calm, almost nonchalant tone.

"At school," I said.

"That's just a nasty word that some white people call black people," she explained.

Mom was trying hard not to show how upset she was. The word seemed to have a frightening power behind it. She was stern as she said, "Brenda, the next time he calls you anything other than your name, just ignore him. Walk away. And go tell your teacher."

Well, that was easier said than done. Grover continued to taunt me every chance he got and this went on for weeks. He would tell me I was ugly, stupid, a black nigger bitch. This was when he caught me alone. In front of other kids, he would make fun of everything about me – my face, my hair, my clothes, and my skin color. On the playground, he would run past me and yell in my ear, and sometimes threw dirt and rocks at me. I did my best to avoid him. I remember one day I was playing on the monkey bars and out of the corner of my eye, spotted him coming in my direction. I ran to the bathroom and hid there until recess was over.

I had always liked school and liked being around the other children. But I began to dread going because I was afraid Grover would hurt me. That day came when Grover was running past me on the playground and he spit in my face. His spit still sliding down my face, I ran to tell the teacher.

She handed me a tissue and said, "Wipe it off and start lining up. It's time to go inside." That was it, just get in line.

Nothing happened to Grover. It was as if the teacher was all right with him spitting in my face. This was one of my most hurtful and embarrassing moments as a little girl. That day I wasn't just a little girl, I was a little black girl.

Again, I felt different, a theme that seemed to emerge constantly throughout my childhood. Those feelings were only magnified when, in the fifth grade, a teacher moved me and the one other black student, Debbie, to the back of the class, apart from the other children. I could tell that the teacher didn't like us. The only explanation I could come up with was that she didn't like us because we were black. On one occasion we were told to go out into the hallway because she didn't like the way we smelled. As our classmates stared and some laughed, we got up and walked out of the classroom to sit in the hallway.

Aside from being isolated from the other students, the move to the back of the classroom had other implications. One day, I asked this teacher to help me with a math problem she had written on the chalk board.

"I've already explained it once," she said in an icy tone. "I'm not going to explain it again."

"But I can't see the board from here," I protested.

She ignored me. I still remember the way her hair looked – gray, and she wore it up in a bun. I just stared at that bun for several moments, trying to calm myself down from the hurt she had thrown at me. This could be the reason why math has always been my worst subject.

My parents went to school to talk to the teacher. I waited out in the hallway while they met. She told them that the other black girl and I were dirty and that we smelled. My mother almost lost her temper right then and there. We didn't have a lot of money to spare, but we never went to school dirty or smelly. My mother and father were both offended.

Grover's racism could have been dismissed as the foolish behavior of a mean-spirited child. But when racism comes from a teacher, it carries an extra weight. Teachers have an aura of authority. Their words, actions and attitudes have a great influence on students. This was the last straw for my parents, and they made the decision to move me to South Beaver School. Before the start of my sixth-grade school year, my parents took me out of NAU Elementary and enrolled me at the neighborhood school, South Beaver Elementary School. South Beaver was a stark contrast to NAU Elementary in the sense that it was primarily ethnic. Almost all of the students were black, Hispanic, or Native American. Suddenly, my skin color didn't set me apart.

Odd then, what really made South Beaver a breath of fresh air for me was another white teacher. His name was Mr. Cromer. Six feet tall, with sandy blond hair and wire rimmed glasses, Mr. Cromer was a very loving and gentle spirit. He was, quite simply, the best teacher I ever had.

Fair and approachable, he was committed to making sure that every student had the chance to get a great education. He always looked for ways to help all students learn. If a student didn't understand something, Mr. Cromer would take as much time as necessary to ensure that the student caught on. He was unfailingly patient, compassionate and understanding, constantly telling us how much he cared for us and how important we all were. He told us that each and every one of us could be anything that we wanted to be, which, for a group of children from the south side of Flagstaff, was important.

Unfortunately, it didn't take too long for me to figure out that even at South Beaver, I was somehow different.

I didn't know it at the time, but my years at NAU Elementary had insulated me from the culture of my neighborhood. NAU was largely white and mostly middle-class to upper-middle class. South Beaver, on the other hand, was ethnic and most likely considered poor. At NAU, I never remember seeing a fight. At South Beaver, kids fought at the drop of a hat. It was a tough school in a tough neighborhood. Even the girls had an aura of fierceness about them and I was, at once, intimidated.

My parents had always put great emphasis on speaking proper English. As my mother said, "Your name will get to Phoenix before you do," meaning that people pay more attention to what a person does than to what he or she says. And so, my siblings and I were taught to watch how we spoke so that people didn't think we lacked common sense or an education. Slang and cursing were just not acceptable in our home.

But when I got to South Beaver, I was exposed to a whole new vocabulary. Kids cursed profusely and they spoke a form of slang that was not acceptable in my home. At first, I was determined to adapt. I tried to cuss and talk ghetto. But I wasn't good at it or even comfortable. It went against my family's values. It didn't take long for me to willingly give that up.

As I progressed through junior high school and into high school, I felt more and more isolated.

Some of the black students accused me of "acting white," not only because of my speech, but because of the way I dressed. My mom was a pretty good seamstress and made a lot of our clothes. In fact, she was probably too good at that craft because a lot of the kids assumed that we were wealthy, mainly because of the quality of clothes we wore. At least that is what a few girls told me.

In 1977, just as I was starting Flagstaff High School, my parents bought a home in Fort Valley Estates, which was located on the north side of town and was a very nice and quiet neighborhood in Flagstaff. It was a beautiful home and we were the first black family to move into that neighborhood. That fact didn't go unnoticed among my peers. I was living with white people, the story went.

So there I was, a black girl who talked "white," dressed "white" and lived in a "white" neighborhood. I began to realize that not all prejudices are based on skin color.

No matter what, I always wound up on the outside, it seemed.

I had white friends, but we were just school friends. I was never invited to their homes to visit or for parties. The girls I was close to in high school – Cynthia, Debbie, and Laura – were black like me.

I became very hard on myself. More and more, I retreated to my music, which was about the only aspect of my young life that I felt confident about. Shy, and unable to express my feelings in conversation, I channeled my emotions into the songs I would write, songs I never shared with anyone else. I began to dream of being a famous songwriter/singer. People would like me then. They would want to be around me, admire me. It was my escape, my sanctuary.

During recess, when the other children were outside playing and forming friendships, I would seclude myself in the music room, where I could sit and play the piano. My sixth grade teacher, Mr. Cromer, would often peek in the doorway of the music room and encourage me to go out and play with the other children. But I preferred to keep to myself.

By my junior year in high school, I had pretty much given up fitting into the social scene at school. Music was about my only source of joy by then and I immersed myself into the school's music programs, playing in the marching band, the jazz band, symphony, and orchestra.

I played the piano, the drums, cymbals, bells, and the xylophone. I was a singer then but only at church. Even there my lack of self-esteem began to limit me. Other band members recognized my ability and encouraged me to try out for solos, but I still felt inadequate. Although I loved every moment of it including the practicing before, during, and after school, I didn't believe I could play as well as everyone said I did.

However, making music was an amazing escape for me. I felt as if I was in another world when I was playing. When I was in high school band I dreamed about playing in a college band. While I was in the symphony I saw myself playing for a beautiful ballet at Radio City Music Hall. I used my imagination and dreamed about writing songs that would change the world and affect people in a positive way. Songs that would inspire people and make a difference. I saw myself traveling and singing all over the world, in every venue – church, stage, radio, and television.

One day when I was in 6th grade during lunch break, I was at my accustomed piano stool in the music room, when I sensed that someone was watching me. I looked up to see a boy standing in the doorway. He didn't say a word. He just stood there in the doorway listening to me play the piano.

For the next several days, he would stand in the doorway and watch me play. A few days later, he walked into the room and sat down in a chair not far from the piano. Each day, he moved a little closer until, finally, I found him sitting beside me on the piano stool.

His name was Stanley. Much later, he would turn out to be the first of many fun, adventurous, challenging, destructive romantic relationships. But back then, he was just a sweet boy who befriended me. And I was in need of a friend.

Chapter 3
"Let the Music Play"

When I am playing any instrument, or singing, or writing a song, I am completely at peace. I am able to get out of my problems and issues and simply listen to the voice inside me that confirms I am good enough. However, as high school drew to a close, even the music was not enough to illuminate my darkening world. I just wanted to be finished with school and move on with my life, even though I had no real plan for my future apart from the dreams I began to realize would probably never come true. I didn't believe in myself.

One day I happened to overhear a conversation between two girls. One of the girls mentioned that she was going to go to summer school so that she could earn enough credits to graduate early and enroll in college in January.

I approached the girl and asked her where I could get information about the summer school program. It seemed like a perfect idea: I'd go to summer school, graduate in December and enroll at NAU for the spring term.

After getting all the information together, I approached my parents with the idea. They agreed. I attended summer school at Coconino High school. By the end of the summer, I had acquired enough credits for a full semester and graduated from Flagstaff High school in December, a semester ahead of my classmates.

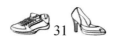

It seemed like a good idea at the time. But it didn't take long for me to realize that I wasn't prepared to be a college student.

For one thing, I was terribly shy and unsure of myself. In fact, just going through registration seemed overwhelming. Even though I hadn't made many close friends in high school, there was some comfort to being around familiar faces. But at NAU, I rarely saw a familiar face. I felt desperately alone and completely out of place.

I thought there would be someone to help me figure out my class schedule, but if those people existed, I was far too shy to ask for their help and no one was just willing to help me either. I also didn't go to my parents with this, especially because I had been so insistent on graduating early. So I wound up taking too heavy a load. I dropped my math and science classes soon after the term began.

College, I soon discovered, was much different from high school and it wasn't long before I began to regret my decision to graduate early.

Sometimes I'd run into my high school classmates and listen as they talked about school – the crazy things the boys did, what happened on the school bus or in the cafeteria. They talked about their plans for the prom and graduation and it sounded so exciting.

By contrast, my school days were spent sitting in lecture halls among strangers. High school, even for me, was a lot more fun than college, I found out.

My lack of maturity, along with my laundry list of insecurities, made college courses all the more difficult. It wasn't long before I began to lose interest. About the only class that held my attention was piano recital and I began to spend hours and hours in the recital hall. I had a great piano instructor who really pushed me to read music and learn. I was grateful for the attention she gave me, so I poured myself into the classical pieces she had chosen for me, a genre I had never been exposed to.

The recital was held on a week-day and my parents were at work. On the day of my recital, I waited nervously for my performance. When my name was called, my teacher whispered "Relax. You'll do fine."

And I did. I'll never forget the piece – Beethoven's "Fur Elise." When I had finished, my teacher was thrilled and I began to feel the warm glow of achievement.

About that time, the girls at my high school were busy preparing for senior prom. Although I was a college student, I was still eligible to participate in the prom with my class. I hoped that Stanley, who was as close to being a boyfriend as anyone, would ask me to the prom. I waited for him to ask because I surely didn't have the nerve to approach him. He must have felt the same way. He never asked. Another boy asked me to go to prom, but I didn't want to go with him. So I missed my senior prom altogether.

Fortunately, the disappointment of prom gave way to the promise of graduation ceremonies and the blur of activities associated with graduation put me in a much better state of mind.

When my name was called at the class of 1980 graduation ceremony, I felt a burst of pride. Suddenly, I was in the spotlight, just for a moment, like all my other classmates of course. But in that moment, I felt special.

The ceremony ended it was all hugs and laughter and talk of plans and "let's stay in touch."

The euphoria carried over to the graduation party at the Elks Lodge, but it didn't last. My parents, who neither

smoked nor drank, were extremely uncomfortable in the night-club setting and I was ill at-ease in their presence.

We didn't stay at the Elks Lodge very long, which was Okay with me. After all, there was another party, this one just for the graduates. That was the party I was looking forward to.

As we were leaving, I told my parents about the party, assuming I'd be allowed to attend. You only graduate high school once, after all. To my horror, my parents didn't think it was a good idea to go because it was already late. I sat in the back seat of the car fuming as we drove home. When we got home, I stomped off to my bedroom and started to get undressed. I could hear the two of them in the other room, talking.

A moment later, Mom came into my room and asked if I really wanted to go to the party. But I was too far gone by then. I was really upset. "No!" I said emphatically and went to bed.

I do not remember if that was the night that I decided to move out on my own. But I do know that it soon became my secret goal.

When you don't have a social life to speak of, it leaves plenty of time for other things. My outlet was work. I held hostess and waitress jobs at local restaurants during all my high school years. I never minded work, really. A work ethic was something my parents taught us at an early age and I enjoyed working and making my own money.

So I began to save my money for the day I could move out on my own. Shortly after my 18th birthday, just as fall classes at NAU began, I had enough money to rent a studio apartment near campus.

Saturday morning the five of us were in the kitchen, cleaning up from breakfast. I was so nervous I felt dizzy, but

sputtered out anyway, "I found a really nice place near campus, and I can afford the rent on it."

My dad, who had been halfway out the door, stopped in his tracks and turned to look at me. My mother kept on rinsing the dishes. Her voice was clear and steady as she said, "That's a big responsibility, Brenda. And it's dangerous living on your own."

"Aw, Carrie, she's old enough," my dad said. I looked from one to the other. I assured my mother that I would take that responsibility seriously and that I really felt ready to make the move. This discussion didn't earn my mother's nod of approval, but after a few more conversations during the two weeks that followed, they both accepted my decision.

The apartment I found was a studio in a converted trailer complex called Chateau Royal. My mother didn't like the place, but allowed me to go ahead. When the big day came, I happily packed my things into my car. What couldn't fit into my car went into my parents' car. Dwight and Sharon rode with us as we took both vehicles to Chateau Royal.

I couldn't wait for my brother and sister, who were by then 15 and 14, to see my apartment. I'd spoken with them earlier about maybe staying overnight with me that first night, and they seemed excited about the prospect. My parents were not too keen on the idea, though, but I hadn't given up hope.

We arrived, and I retrieved my front door key from the manager. The place was not nearly as clean as we kept our home. My mother helped me wipe down some of the surfaces and talked to me about where things could go, while my father, with Dwight and Sharon, unloaded my belongings from the cars. Once that was done, I asked my siblings to stay the night.

They looked at Mom to see if she would agree.

She shook her head. "Get in the car."

They filed out. Mom told me goodbye and shut the door behind her.

I stood there in the living room for a moment, wondering what had just happened. I wanted to fling open the door and run after them and ask her why but I didn't move. I just stood there in the room, feeling hurt. As bad as I wanted my mother's approval, I was determined to live my own life and be my own person.

My parents and siblings eventually got used to me living on my own. I settled into my little apartment and felt like a real adult. It was such a great feeling to get up in the morning, take a shower, get dressed, eat breakfast and head off to work.

I had started working at Security Pacific Bank as a teller and I really loved the job. The car my parents had bought for me soon began to give me trouble, so I started looking for a car I could afford. Looking through the newspaper, I saw a classified ad for a green two-door 1968 Pontiac. It wasn't much to look at. In fact, it was covered in dust and seemed as though it hadn't been driven in years.

But after a test drive and an inspection that didn't reveal any mechanical defects, I decided to buy the car. I gave the man $350. He gave me the title. Buying a car with my own money was another first in the life of an independent young woman.

I immediately drove my "new" car to my parents' house. Dwight and Sharon crawled through the beat-up interior and examined the various dents on the exterior. We agreed on a name for my new car– "Mula" – and we took off down the street, radio blasting, laughing and shouting and making a point to hail anybody we knew to show off the car.

Mula had more than her share of dents, rips and defects. She had a big hole in the muffler, which announced my presence a few blocks ahead of my arrival. Even so, I loved that car. I doubt I'll ever have a car that evokes the feelings that first one of my very own produced.

Life was good. I had a job I enjoyed. I had my own apartment and my car.

I also had something else I'd never had: Friends and freedom. This was new.

I met a few girls at NAU and we began to hang out together, either at their dorm rooms or at my apartment. We started going out to bars and clubs, drinking and dancing and being young and carefree.

A few of us formed a little singing group and sometimes we would practice at the NAU music hall. We never performed anywhere, though. It was strictly something we did for the fun of it. Sometimes we would have daiquiri or margarita parties that would last all night. None of us were into drugs, but we did drink a lot.

The combination of work and having fun with my friends altered my priorities. I would miss a class or two, then drop the class when I fell behind. Before long, I had dropped out of school completely.

It didn't take long until my primary focus was on having fun, almost as if I was trying to make up for all the parties and freedom I had never enjoyed when I was living with my parents.

I look back on that time now and realize that I was not very well equipped for the amount of independence I was given. Before moving out on my own, I really never had much experience making choices; most of my choices were made for me. Suddenly, I was faced with a broad range of options: Do I go out tonight? Or do I stay in? Do I drink tonight? Do I hang out with this group of people?

There were too many choices. As starved as I had been for close friendship, I was incapable of making well-reasoned decisions about my relationships. So I did what I had always done in those situations: I left the decision-making to someone else. If the group decided to set their hair on fire and jump off the bridge, I was looking for the lighter. So, really, I wasn't making choices. Up until that point, my parents had made my choices for me. Now, it was my friends who were making the choices for me. I was just along for the ride.

It was a pretty safe ride at that point, though. My life then probably wasn't much different than that of any other young woman in her early 20s. Although having fun was a huge priority, and I was no longer going to school, I was still going to work, and paying my bills. I also continued to go to church and play the piano.

Sometimes, though, a life can turn on a single thought. Any bad act begins first with a thought.

And the thought that came to me didn't suggest even a hint of danger. I just happened to think of Stanley, that sweet boy who I had known since sixth grade.

When we were in high school, Stanley and I talked about dating and writing music together and pursuing our dreams. But when I went to NAU, we sort of drifted apart. We didn't stay in touch, but from time to time I'd hear about him through mutual friends.

Stanley had moved to Tucson. On the spur of the moment, I decided to go down to Tucson and surprise him. My parents knew I was going, but I didn't tell them why. They would have never approved of my being so forthright as to look up an old friend like that. An old boyfriend, even more so.

It was not the best decision either but it was the first in a series of choices that would ultimately lead to a life of addiction and homelessness.

I have no way of knowing for certain how things would have turned out if I had not made the decision to rekindle my relationship with Stanley. All I do know is that re-uniting with Stanley was my introduction to drugs. Stanley did not cause my addiction; I own that. But this is where I was introduced to marijuana and a guide into a world I wish I had never wandered into.

Of course, I never imagined that visiting Stanley would be a turning point in my life. All I knew is that I missed my friend and that it would be great to see him.

I had planned to go to Tucson just for the weekend. After all, I had to be at work on Monday morning. While I was gone, I let a few of my girlfriends stay at my place, just to keep an eye on things.

Butterflies fluttered in my stomach when I knocked on the door of Stanley's apartment. I wondered if I was doing the right thing.

Greg one of Stanley's roommates, answered the door. Stanley, Greg and Mel, were sharing the apartment. Greg and Mel were from Flagstaff, too, and we all went to school together.

Greg told me that Stanley was at work and since I had left my car in Flagstaff, Mel offered to drive me to see him. Stanley was shocked to see me, I could tell. We talked for a few minutes, and I agreed to meet him at his apartment when he got off of work that evening.

To pass the time, Mel and I went to a local bar. By the time Stanley got home, we were both pretty drunk.

We all sat in the living room of his apartment and talked about the old times in Flagstaff and listening to music. Then one of the boys pulled out a shoe box.

Although I had never smoked weed before, I knew what marijuana looked like and smelled like. Mel rolled up a big joint, lit it and began passing it around.

When it came my way the first time, I passed. I was afraid I would overdose and die. They finished the joint then we all ran out to the store for snacks. When we returned, they lit another joint. Again, I declined when the joint came my way. The boys kept telling me that I should at least give it a try and I finally relented. I took a draw on the joint and immediately began to cough and choke, which the boys thought was pretty funny.

I didn't experience the high the boys had said I would feel. All I felt was the burn in my lungs. After a couple more drinks, I tried it again and although I choked a bit, at last I began to feel the effects of the weed. It wasn't so much a high to me as it was a very relaxing sensation. The more I smoked, the more relaxed I felt.

Soon, we began to pass out. Stanley and I slept side by side on the couch, Mel on the other couch, and Greg in his room. We spent the next day smoking. Again, the weed created a sense of relaxation. It was a peaceful, laid-back feeling. I really liked that feeling, I realized. The weed kept coming and I kept smoking. A weekend visit turned into a two-week stay. I was fired from my job at the bank. Somehow, that didn't really matter, though.

While I was down in Tucson taking the accelerated course in "How to be a pothead," my apartment-sitting friends in Flagstaff were making a wreck of my place, eating everything in the house, making tons of long-distance calls on my phone and having party after party. My mom found out and called Stanley.

"Put her on the next bus to Flagstaff," she said tersely.

My parents were there to meet me when the bus arrived. It was not a happy reunion. I spent the ride to my apartment trying to figure out what to say to them while they spent the ride biting their tongues.

My parents helped me clean up the wreckage that had once been my apartment. While they were doing so, they said to me the things they felt I needed to hear. I can still remember my mother's comments. 'Brenda, you're not living your life the right way. How do you expect God's going to bless you if you aren't doing the right thing?" She was right, of course. But I couldn't see it back then.

My father didn't say much, but he didn't have to. His few words spoke volumes. "You know better, Rena. You're selling yourself short, plain and simple." Unfortunately, I wasn't capable of really listening to either one of them at that point.

I did realize that I had two options: I could either A. start making better choices or B. do a better job of covering my tracks. I chose Option B.

It was shortly after that when I plunged with head-first enthusiasm into the party scene. Having fun became my only real aspiration. My parents were unable to stop me. The one thing I didn't abandon was my dream of having a career in music. Between parties, I managed to put together an all-girl singing group and we weren't half bad. We entered local talent shows and walked away with prizes ranging from gift certificates at restaurants to trips to Las Vegas.

But that was about the extent of my ambitions. Before long, I began to lose interest even in music. I went from job to job, making enough money to support my party lifestyle, but I began to encounter some red flags – extreme headaches, major hangovers, and finally black-outs. I was in trouble.

I lost jobs as a result of my lifestyle, but I was always able to find a new one. Of course, each subsequent job was worse than the previous. I kept moving from apartment to apartment as my income decreased. Finally, I lived with my cousin Tracy in a little motel room apartments and continued to party.

By then Mel had moved back to Flagstaff and we began to spend a lot of time together, mainly drinking and smoking weed.

An opportunity to get out of that rut came when a couple of my roommates made plans to move to Phoenix. They wanted me to come so we all made plans to make the move. I had a few months to get ready and I had intended to save enough money to get set up when we got to Phoenix. But when the time for the move came, I didn't have any money. I had used it all on weed and alcohol. My friends offered to take care of my expenses until I got a job in Phoenix, but I didn't like the idea of relying on them for that.

So I stayed in Flagstaff while my friends moved to Phoenix. Mel and I stayed there in that shabby little house in Flagstaff, listening to Prince, drinking and getting high. Soon, we became a couple and we began to make plans to move out of the hovel we were living in and into a real apartment. But there was a time management issue that complicated those plans. Namely, when most of your day is devoted to lying around and smoking weed, you run out of time to do more ambitious things.

We found a temporary solution. One of my old roommates had ordered a box of checks for her checking account before moving to Phoenix, and must have forgotten to cancel the order. All I know is that the checks arrived in the mail one day and soon Mel and I were writing checks all over the place.

The mother of my friend, Mrs. Fletcher who had ordered the checks soon began to get phone calls about the bad checks her daughter was suddenly writing. Mrs. Fletcher came to see us at the shack. She told us what was happening. I was very ashamed, so I went with her to the police station and turned myself in. The police took my statement, arrested me, took my finger prints and released me. Because it was my first arrest, I was placed in a diversion program.

But I was too far gone by then. I didn't complete the program and was put on probation.

A lot of people turn their lives around when they are put on probation. I wasn't one of those people, though.

I didn't like having to report to a probation officer and resented the power the P.O. had over my life. Over the next few years, I had several probation officers and soon realized that there is nothing better than having a supportive P.O. – and nothing worse than having a P.O. who takes a disliking to you.

As part of my probation, I was ordered to attend a 12-Step program. This is a tricky subject, for me. I recognize that programs such as Alcoholics Anonymous have been enormously successful for many, many people. But I can't say that was my experience. Frankly, I hated those A.A. meetings. The meetings I attended always seemed to be full of chain-smoking people who spent most of the program swapping "war stories" from their time as addicts. I also hated the idea of having to tell the group that you were an addict or an alcoholic. To me, that was an intensely personal subject.

Of course, my experience with A.A. was greatly colored by my attitude. At that point, all I really wanted to do was to get through probation without going to jail again. Making the sort of changes that would help me become a productive member of the community wasn't much of a priority, to be honest.

I stopped visiting my parents except on occasion. Instead of seeing them, I would call them on the phone to check in. They pretty much knew what was going on with me, and they were heartbroken. They would plead and cajole me to change my ways. My mother tried to appeal to my responsibility to family. She told me, "There is nothing your dad wouldn't do for you, Brenda. Do you know what your behavior is doing to him? Your brother and sister look up to you. Do you know what kind of example this is setting for them?"

My life then was all about partying and having fun. Neither the sort of life my parents presented, nor the sort of life A.A. presented were my idea of fun. A life that didn't include drinking and smoking weed could not be fun at all. Beyond that, I had a lot of resentment about my situation. On one level, I recognized that I had done something wrong and had to be accountable for it. But I also felt that three years of probation, paying restitution, and going to programs like A.A. were excessive and unfair. I didn't accept responsibility for my actions and recognize the part I played in my own situation.

So my goal was to work the system.

Take it from someone who knows: You can't win when that's your attitude. That's a lesson that took me quite a few years and several trips to jail to finally realize. Although I made a half-hearted attempt to follow the rules, I soon returned to the party scene. Mel and I soon broke up and I moved in with Cindy who was a co-worker and eventually a good friend. Cindy and I were both waitresses and like me, she too liked to party.

I grew especially close to Cindy who shared a lot of my bad habits. We both enjoyed smoking weed, drinking and taking acid. Cindy had one other vice that I soon began to share: Shoplifting; or "shopping" as we called it.

Our main motivation for stealing was for the thrill it provided. We would go to the mall and start at the JC Penney Store and work our way through the mall. We would steal clothes, jewelry and shoes and put them in a shopping bag. When the bag was filled, we would leave and put the stolen items in the car then return for more.

It was an incredibly stupid, dangerous thing to do for someone who was already on probation, of course. It flew in the face of all the ethical principles on which I had been raised. And I knew it. But shoplifting was another type of high. Back then, I was all for any high I could get.

One night Cindy and I went to a little bar and began drinking. We went outside to smoke some weed and later decided to go to a convenience store, where we stole a fifth of Jim Beam and a six-pack of soda. We had money; that wasn't the issue. Somehow, stealing the items was far more fun.

As we were leaving the store, two employees grabbed us and held us until the police arrived. We were booked. Cindy was released the following morning. But for me, the consequences were more severe. The shoplifting charge was a violation of my probation, so I spent a week in jail.

Going to jail for a week would have been another excellent opportunity for me to do some soul-searching, maybe alter the arc of my life. And I did quit shoplifting. But I wasn't about the quit drinking and smoking weed.

In the span of just a couple of years, I had gone from being a well-adjusted young woman who was working and going to school and looking forward to a bright future to a woman who succumbed to addiction. I had lost my little apartment, a good job, the respect of my family and was becoming uncomfortably familiar with the inside of a jail cell.

And it would only get worse.

 45

Chapter 4
"Me, A Drug Addict?"

One afternoon I came home early from work to find Stanley, with whom I was living by then, and Mel in the back room smoking something out of a glass pipe.

They seemed startled to see me.

"What is that?" I asked.

"It's crack, girl," Stanley said.

"Want some?" Mel asked.

Of course, I thought it through…for about two seconds, anyway.

They put a small piece of the white rock on the screen of the glass pipe, lit it, I put my lips to the opening of the pipe and took a draw.

Whoa! The cocaine coursed through my body, instantly creating a high altogether different from the laid-back high of smoking weed and far more immediate than the kick you get from alcohol.

With alcohol and weed, I had experienced something of a novice period. But by the end of that day, I was an expert on crack cocaine. I quickly discovered that even a $50 rock doesn't last nearly long enough, especially when it is divided among three people. As our supply of the precious commodity disappeared up the glass pipe, we began cutting the rock into smaller and smaller pieces. When it was all gone, Mel and

Stanley began scraping out the inside of the pipe and smoking that.

When it was obvious that it was all gone, I became restless, agitated. I looked at Mel. I looked at Stanley. I started thinking about whether they had given me my fair share. Men!

They must have sensed this somehow.

"Hey, you want to go and cop some more?" one of them suggested.

I reached into my apron pocket for my tip money. There was eighty dollars, money I had intended to spend on frivolous things like groceries, gas, the electric bill, etc.

We went to the dope house and bought another $20 rock. I don't know what we were thinking. We returned to the apartment, smoked the $20, went back to the dope house and got some more. We kept doing this until the money was gone.

I used to wonder how things might have been different if I hadn't come home early from work that day. But excuses look a lot like reasons when you are an addict. And none of them make any difference anyway.

What really mattered was that, from the moment I took that first hit on the crack pipe, I spent the next several years chasing a high that could never be found again.

I didn't smoke crack again until about a week later. Stanley and Mel picked me up from work that day and we went directly to the crack house. I had expected to get the same rush as before, but quickly learned what every addict learns – there's no high like the first high. I figured it was just a matter of smoking more crack, that if I could smoke enough I'd find that old magic.

Before long, crack was about the only thing I could really focus on. It wasn't long before I realized that I didn't need to

have Stanley or Mel with me when I wanted to smoke crack. Sometimes, I got high by myself; sometimes I'd get high with my "new" friends. I was surprised to find out that a lot of my friends and acquaintances had already discovered this drug.

It didn't take long for me to experience some of its side effects. For one thing, my senses intensified. I would hear and see things in the room that weren't there. I began to believe the police were after me, that they were watching me and listening in on my phone conversations. I was convinced that police had installed listening devices in my apartment, my car and at my work. Before long, I convinced myself that the dope man was really an undercover cop and that he was going to arrest me as soon as I bought crack from him.

The paranoia did nothing to diminish my appetite for the drug, though. I began to work extra shifts so that I'd have more money to spend on my habit. Crack was soon the dominating influence of my life. Often, I would work double-shifts and head straight for the dope house after getting off. I'd stay all night at the dope house, smoking, until it was time to go to work the next day. I'd arrive at work having had no sleep, not having even taken a shower, wearing the same clothes I had worn the previous day.

In a matter of a few weeks, my relationship with Stanley and Mel had turned ugly, and I attribute most of that to crack. Getting high with them together became almost impossible. They would hide dope from me or each other and we all played head games. They grew increasingly possessive with the crack pipe, which always became the tipping point. Stanley and Mel would get into arguments over crack and sometimes I'd be right in the middle of it, fighting like a wild woman.

It reached the point where we couldn't stand to be around one another. By then Stanley was living elsewhere, and Mel had a place in the same apartment complex I did. However crack can make you be very forgiving especially if it means you get to smoke more of it. They still came over to smoke. One night Mel and I had a particularly nasty fight and I threw him out of my apartment. Stanley had already gone. I called my father and asked him to accompany me home from work, because I was afraid. We arrived at my place to find that the door of my apartment had been forced open. I stayed near the door while my dad looked around to find out what had happened. He found Mel hiding in my closet. I told him he had to get out, and called the police. My dad's presence was the only thing that kept him from attacking me, I think. The cops showed up and made Mel leave.

After things settled down, I went back to the dope house and got high. When I returned the next day, I happened to notice a pair of shoes lying by the trash dumpster that looked like a pair I had. I picked them up and realized they were, indeed, my shoes.

"That's strange," I thought. On an impulse I looked into the dumpster and was stunned to see all of my shoes and a lot of other things from my apartment.

I ran upstairs and found the door wide open and my apartment in shambles. I knew immediately that Mel was the culprit. I walked over to his apartment and knocked on his door, but he wouldn't answer.

Again, I called the cops. Mel wouldn't answer the door for the cops, either. Finally, they broke open the door and found Mel in his apartment. While the cops were trying to sort everything out, the garbage truck arrived to empty the dumpsters. After the police finished taking my statement, I went to the dumpster to retrieve my stuff. The dumpster was empty. I had lost all of my shoes and a lot of other possessions. This was the first time I lost my shoes.

I told myself that I had to make some changes, including giving up crack. I moved back in with my parents, who were loving and cautiously optimistic. Their acceptance gave me courage. The first night we sat down to eat dinner together, my mother closed her eyes, held my hand tight and said, "Thank you, God. Praise Jesus, for bringing my daughter home." Never letting go of my hand, she opened her eyes and looked straight at me, "Now, Brenda, you have the opportunity for a fresh start. Whatever you want, you can do it."

I tried. I began to focus more on my work. I was enrolled in Beauty School at the time. My plan was to work, finish up Beauty School and get on with my life.

I still went out to the clubs. I drank, I smoked some weed, but I stayed away from the crack.

How naïve I was. Obviously, walking away from crack isn't a simple matter of deciding you're going to quit or at least it wasn't for me. Crack was always on my mind. I missed the rush. I often dreamed about it, to the point where I could smell it in my dreams. But for a while, I managed to keep that monster at bay.

Soon, I finished school and got an internship at a barbershop. I learned to sew in weaves and fit toupees as I waited to get certification to take the state board exam. But through it all, the call of crack grew stronger and stronger. I couldn't resist it any more. My parents had no idea how bad it had really gotten.

When I look back on those days, I'm amazed that I managed to stay out of jail as long as I did. I had been on probation for more than two years and yet I always managed to get clean just long enough to pass drug tests that were a part of my probation.

But you can only dodge so many bullets. My luck ran out during a visit with my probation officer, who handed me a little plastic cup and sent me off to produce a urine sample. A big lump rose in my throat and my heart began to pound. I knew that my urine would come back positive for cocaine this time, which would be a violation of my probation. I was headed to jail.

I did the only thing I could think of. I dipped the cup in the toilet, filled it with water and returned to the probation officer. I figured it would at least buy me some time.

I went home and tried all the tricks I had heard about from other addicts to get the cocaine out of my system. I drank vinegar. I took supplements that were rumored to mask the presence of cocaine. None of this worked, of course. The only way to avoid failing a test is not to use and, of course, in my distorted mind, not using was simply not an option.

Predictably, the day of reckoning came with a knock on the door at my parents' home. It was my probation officer. I tried to think up some new lies to tell her, but when your urine sample comes back as water, that's a pretty hard thing to explain away. I was forced to provide another sample, which came back positive for cocaine. I was arrested on the spot, right in front of my mother.

I'll never forget seeing my mom breaking down as the police put me in handcuffs and led me out to a squad car. I was headed to jail.

I served just thirty days of a six-month sentence in jail, and the rest I spent on work release. I would get out of jail at 7 a.m. and be required to return 12 hours later. The ability to escape jail for 12 hours a day made my situation fairly tolerable. I worked at the barbershop and went to my parents' house afterwards until it was time to report back. I still attended church on Sundays, so in some respects I managed to live a fairly normal life.

One of the aspects of living in a small town is that no matter where you are you're not likely to be among strangers. This was true even at jail. Many members of the jail staff were people I went to high school with, which earned me a little better treatment. One of the female guards and I had grown up together, so when I returned to jail in the evening, I would accompany her on her rounds before finally going to my cell. I also was able to make phone calls and receive phone calls, even though it was against official policy.

One night as I was making the rounds with my guard friend I ran into an attorney who was there to consult with a client. He was a tall white man with long hair and a beard. He introduced himself as Lee Phillips, a public defender. We only talked for a couple of minutes, but he was very polite and seemed pretty nice.

The next day I was surprised when a guard came to my cell and told me I had a visitor. I couldn't imagine who that would be since I was on work release. The guard led me to a room where inmates go to consult with their attorneys.

Sitting in the chair across the small desk was Lee Phillips. He opened his briefcase, retrieved a hamburger from one of the local fast-food places and offered it to me. I gladly accepted the gift – until you've had a steady diet of jail food, you aren't likely to understand what a treat a fast-food burger can be.

Of course, I still didn't know the purpose of his visit; I had never had him as a public defender and had only met him a day earlier. I just sat and happily consumed the burger, waiting for him to clue me in.

He said he had read some of my court file and felt he could get me out of jail. He told me he was going to file a motion to that effect right away, and that he would represent me in court. I was thrilled.

When I returned to my cell and told some of the other women what had happened, they didn't believe me. That was understandable, I thought, but there was something about Lee Phillips that gave me confidence. The next morning I left on work release and went immediately to tell my parents the good news before going to work.

Sure enough, Lee called me at work later that afternoon and told me I was being released from jail. When I returned to the jail that evening, they released me. I gathered my personal effects and went home.

Of course, I still faced court charges for the probation violation. But Lee went to work on that, too. He hired an investigator to help with my case and began assembling witnesses who would testify on my behalf. Lee was confident I'd be released from probation and walk out of court a free woman. I was hopeful.

The day came for court and people from my church, my work and family members testified on my behalf. As I listened to Lee make his argument, I was amazed. I had had public defenders before. Generally, I didn't have much confidence in their ability to do what was best for me.

Lee was different in every way.

When both the prosecution and defense had made their arguments, the judge began to review the two arguments. I looked at Lee, who listened attentively and seemed to have an aura of complete confidence.

Finally, the judge announced his decision. I had completed my probation. I was a free woman!

An impromptu celebration broke out amongst my family and friends. There were tears and hugs and laughter. We all thanked Lee for what he had done. Then I went home with my family.

At that time, I didn't attach any personal significance to Lee's efforts on my behalf. I just assumed that he was a very good lawyer doing what a good lawyer is supposed to do. But soon

enough I learned that what Lee really wanted was to broaden my world, build my confidence and encourage my dreams. Ours was, without question, a very healthy relationship; until I ruined it.

Part 2

Chapter 5
"A Whole New World"

A week after my court case ended the phone rang at my parents' home. It was Lee. He said he just wanted to tell me that if I needed anything to give him a call.

"I'm going to New York this week to visit my brother and sisters, but maybe we can get together when I get back and have lunch."

"Uh, yeah," I stammered. "Sure."

Later that week, a postcard from Lee arrived in the mail from New York. As I looked at it, I began to have a funny feeling. My face lit up with a big smile that kept on going for several days. My parents noticed and asked me about it.

I told them about Lee's call and showed them the postcard. They were naturally suspicious. What would a successful white lawyer possibly want to do with a girl like me?

"What does he want?" Mom asked.

"I don't know," I said. And I didn't, but I liked it.

Lee called again when he was back in town, and we made plans to meet for lunch.

We ate at Charlie's Bar in downtown Flagstaff. Lee told me about his trip to New York where his brother and two sisters lived, and filled me in a bit on his background. Raised in rural Ohio, he came to Arizona to work with the Navajo Indians. He built his career working with underrepresented populations, and at the time was preparing to open a private practice after two years in the public defender's office.

I was a little more guarded in what I shared with him from my past. I didn't want to scare him off, after all. So instead, I talked about my dreams of a starting a career in music. He listened attentively and seemed genuinely interested.

When we arrived back at my parents' house, Lee asked if I would go out with again. That was an easy one. "Yes," I said. "I'd like that very much."

I hardly understood what was happening between us. All I knew was that Lee was different than any other man or boyfriend I had ever had. It went well beyond the obvious differences – he was white, 8 years older, well-educated and established in his career.

There was a generosity about him that I had never known in any of my previous relationships. He had also traveled and experienced things that I had only dreamed about.

With Lee I regained the sense of myself that I was missing – the me with dreams, with the belief that nothing was too difficult for me to achieve. I began to rediscover my goals, and my confidence. I felt beautiful.

As our romance blossomed, I was amazed at how attentive Lee was. There was no jealousy, no drama. Even as the more unsavory aspects of my past emerged, he remained kind and understanding. There was not a judgmental bone in this man's body, I realized. Lee was a man I could trust without reservation.

Lee took me to places and exposed me to things that I am sure I would never have experienced otherwise. I have to admit that I liked the lifestyle he enjoyed and shared with me. All of my previous boyfriends were vastly different. Lee treated me like a princess. He was very polite, respectful, and forthright.

We always had a great time no matter what we did or where we went.

Soon, he asked me to move in with him. I immediately said yes, but worried how I would break the news to my parents and how they would respond.

Together Lee and I sat down with my parents, and we explained our feelings for one another. My parents were not sold on the idea completely, but they realized that we were adults and could make those kinds of decisions without their consent. Over time, my parents would grow to love Lee as much as I did. I think they realized what a kind, decent man he was.

We moved in to a beautiful little wooden house in downtown Flagstaff. It was a three bedroom with a front porch and a deck in back. The front bedroom was an office for his law business. Lee pampered me in every way imaginable. We hardly ever cooked; we ate out at nice restaurants for almost every meal. No laundry to do, either. Lee dropped that off to a laundromat each week. We traveled and did fun things all the time. We took trips to San Diego and Washington, D.C. and New York.

Lee was, in some respects, a kindred spirit. Like me, he loved to try new things. He introduced me to different cultures, foods, and lifestyles. I saw my first Broadway musical with him -- *Jelly's Last Jam* – when we traveled to New York. We also went to the *Blue Man Group* at the Public Theater, listened to music at CBGBs. I ate artichokes and Oysters Rockefeller and fried ice cream for the first time in my life in restaurants whose cuisines I had never even known about before, such as Ethiopian, Thai, and Vietnamese, to name a few.

Lee introduced me to his friends, acquaintances, and co-workers. Now I was spending time in the company of judges, attorneys, and accountants. In turn I introduced Lee to Flagstaff's black community, which eventually helped him to build up some of clientele and his practice. I brought him to church, to my parents' house for Easter, Christmas holidays.

There were people, in the white community and the black community, who didn't embrace the relationship because we were an interracial couple. I didn't care what they thought. I was in love and that was all that mattered. It was with Lee that I learned what a healthy, loving relationship was all about. I never had cause to be jealous or suspect him for being unfaithful in any way.

Lee helped me throw a lavish party to celebrate my 30th birthday. The party was held at the home of John Trebon, one of Lee's attorney friends. John helped plan the party, hiring a band to perform. The band I was singing with, Boyz and the Hood also played.

All my friends and family were invited. Walter, my biological dad, and Hazel, came in from Los Angeles for the party. There must have been 200 people there. There was plenty of food and an open bar. It lasted all night.

To me it felt like every party, every prom, every big dance, I had ever missed had been rolled up into one. I'll never forget it.

Lee wasn't simply making a place for me in his world; he actively encouraged me to pursue my own dreams. He wanted me to dream big dreams, to see a bigger world and to find my place in it. With this in mind, he kick-started my music career by introducing me to key people in the music scene and financing my first recording effort, a CD of gospel songs.

I worked as a singer for a number of local bands – the Tommy Dukes Band, followed by Boyz N The Hood, Hot Monte, and Electra Glide. As I look back now, I realize how dangerous my foray into the music world was for me. Until then, I had stayed away from crack cocaine completely. I

honestly felt that drug abuse was nothing more than a painful memory for me. Heck, I didn't even smoke weed, hadn't smoked weed, since I started dating Lee. I did drink, but not like before. Lee was, at most, a social drinker. Alcohol was not a part of our daily life.

But as I immersed myself in the music scene and began to spend more and more time in the company of hard-living musicians, I slowly began a descent into drug abuse. The more I performed, the worse it became.

First, I began to drink more. Then, I began to smoke a little weed every now and then. I justified that by saying that all I had to do was to stay away from crack and I'd be able to handle things.

At first, it was easy to hide it from Lee. But after one fateful night in Tucson, when my beautiful sister friend, Karen and I started snorting lines of cocaine in the ladies room, I fell back head-first into addiction.

It was soon impossible for me to hide my drug abuse from Lee. He could see it in my glassy eyes and erratic behavior whenever I came home high after a gig. It naturally had an effect on our relationship. Lee was alarmed at the turn I was taking, for not only was he strongly opposed to drugs of any kind, but he knew my history. When my addiction got to the point where I began to sell my jewelry and pawn Lee's possessions for money to buy drugs, Lee had had enough. He gave me an ultimatum. I could go into rehab. Or else.

The thought of losing Lee wasn't something I took lightly. Reluctantly, I agreed to go to rehab. The plan was to get clean and resume my singing career.

I found rehab very difficult. Again, I was required to attend A.A. meetings. Again, I hated them.

On the positive side, I did make some friends who seemed genuinely committed to getting sober. My counselor, Margarite, was also a great influence. She was a recovering alcoholic who had lost custody of her children because of her drinking. With her, there was no judgment, only love, wisdom, and support. She could relate to my experiences, because she had lived in some ways, a similar life.

When I completed the program, we had a graduation ceremony. My family and Lee attended and it turned out to be a deeply emotional experience. I remember my mother praying with us during a church service soon afterwards, kneeling down and saying strong and loud, "Thank you, Jesus for removing the taste of crack from my daughter's mouth."

Tragically, for me, something about my relationship with Lee had changed during the whole experience. I had gone into rehab at a very stressful time in Lee's life. He was lead defense counsel in a highly publicized murder trial involving the death of a child. The case was emotionally charged and Lee poured every waking hour into his work. The stress of the trial combined with having a girl friend who was a drug addict going through rehab turned out to be too big a burden for Lee to bear.

Although we tried to pick up where we left off, something important was missing in our relationship. Lee and I both went to counseling together and attended separate counseling, all in hopes that the bonds of trust could be re-established. The pain, the betrayal and disappointment Lee felt were obstacles. For me, feelings of shame over how I had treated Lee rekindled those old fires of self-loathing. I also knew that rehab had not chased away all the demons that haunted me.

I continued to sing with the band, which meant I was always in the vicinity of drugs. I even introduced several band members to crack which made us work harder to get more gigs to earn more money to continue to get high. Performing however was a high in itself. I loved being on stage and singing. The smoke filled rooms brought excitement and the cheering crowds drew me in every time. It was like magic for those few hours. All my troubles disappeared... temporarily. A pattern soon developed. I would relapse, and then go back into treatment. Again and again.

Each time I relapsed, I fell a little deeper. The distance between Lee and I grew. Before long, I was staying out all night. Lee, who was a well-known figure in town, would get calls from the police informing him that his truck was spotted outside a dope house. I often used Lee's truck to transport drugs, drug addicts, and drug dealers around Flagstaff while on my crack binges. I hated what I was doing, but I felt powerless to stop.

I had managed to get a job as a data entry clerk, but my addiction wouldn't allow me to keep the job. I'd pass out at work. Eventually, I was called into the office and told I had to go back into rehab or face being fired. I went into rehab at St. Luke's Hospital in Phoenix for two weeks.

When I got out, I didn't really know where to go. Deep inside, I knew that I had damaged my relationship with Lee beyond repair, but I turned to him in desperation, hoping that somehow, someway I could make it right.

As often as I had betrayed him, for all the pain I had caused, for every time I had returned his good with evil, I loved the man.

So, after signing the release papers, I called my brother, Dwight, who lived in Phoenix and asked if he would buy me a plane ticket for Flagstaff. I wanted to get back home to Lee as soon as possible.

On the short flight home, I thought about how I was going to approach Lee and I rehearsed my speech until the plane touched down. When I got into the terminal, I called Lee's office, but his secretary said that he was in court. I called my mom, who picked me up and drove me to Lee's office.

Lee was on the phone when I arrived, but I could see by his expression that my appearance there was a mistake. His face was a mask of pain and anger. While he was on the phone, I went back to my mom's car to retrieve my bags. As I was walking through the lobby, I ran into Lorenzo who is someone I used to get high with.

I talked to him for a couple of minutes, excused myself, and went to mom's car to get my bags. My Mom was fuming, but she didn't say a word. Looking back I think she was hurt and perhaps even angry with me and the situation. My mom knew my potential but also saw it slipping away from me. I grabbed my bags and went back into the office.

Lorenzo was still in the lobby. He suggested that we get together later at the Monte Vista Lounge, one of our hangouts from the old days.

As I walked away, I began to think about getting high again. I had only been out of rehab for a few hours and suddenly not even my concerns over my tenuous relationship with Lee could prevent me from thinking about smoking crack.

Lee was still on the phone when I returned, so I waited for him in the outer office.

Lee finally ended the phone call and emerged from the office, ready to go home. There was an icy silence between us as he drove home. I was eager to see my two cats, Winnie and Nelson. I was also eager to see the house.

Nothing had changed at home. I took a shower and changed clothes. Lee and I talked for a few minutes, but it was just small talk. I don't think either of us was ready to deal with the ugly truth about our relationship.

Lee said he was going to the gym for a workout and then he was going to work on one of his cases. I told him I was going to go to a Narcotics Anonymous meeting and I'm probably get home around 9 p.m.

I pulled into the parking lot where the Narcotic Anonymous meeting was held, but I couldn't bring myself to get out of the car. I just sat there. Half of me wanted to drive back home, to pour out my heart to Lee and beg for his forgiveness. The other half wanted to meet Lorenzo at the Monte Vista Lounge. The one thing I knew I wasn't going to do was attend that N.A. meeting.

The longer I sat there, the better I liked the idea of going to the bar.

I drove to the bar. As I arrived, I saw two police cars with lights flashing parked outside. So I drove past the bar. It didn't take long to run into one of my crack-smoking pals. I saw Tim at a little store and flagged him down. He jumped into the car and off we went to the nearest ATM, where I withdrew some money.

Finding crack in Flagstaff was no trouble. For a small town, it has an amazingly large drug scene. The next hours were a blur. At some point, another crack buddy, Mikey, wound up in my car and the crack binge continued, with me driving all over the 'hood, buying crack and smoking.

The binge ended the next afternoon when I happened to see my mom's car rolling through the streets. I knew she and my dad were out looking for me. I figured that after I didn't come home, Lee had called them to see if I had spent the night at their house. It was time to go home.

I dropped Mikey off and headed for the house. As I was driving down the street, with my mother and father trailing me in their car, Lee's car pulled into the driveway also.

I went straight to the bathroom to wash up. From that room, I could hear Lee, my mom, and dad discussing what to do. I heard the word "committed" and bolted out into the front room where they were standing together.

Three faces looked at me point blank. Three resolute chins, three pairs of lips drawn tight, each person with sadness in his or her eyes. I knew I had failed the people closest to me in the world, the ones who believed in me the most of all. At this point, what was left to say?

"I'm sorry; I know I let you all down."

No one responded. After a minute, which felt like forever to me, my father stepped close and put his arm around my shoulder. "Rena, you know how much we love you. And how many times we've tried to get you the help you need. To be the support you can rely on." I nodded, tears in my eyes.

"I wish you would listen to good sound advice, Rena, and we keep hoping that one day you will," Mom added. "The truth is, that we've done all we can. *You* have got to straighten up and start living right."

My protests were faint. "I've been trying, Mama, I really have." "Right now we feel deep in our hearts that we just don't have the power to save you. *You* are going to have to pray to the Lord, and ask him to save you. And until you're ready to do that…." her eyes were pools of tears, and she was shaking her head back and forth, back and forth.

"Rena," my dad said and hugged me. "You let us know when you really mean it, and we'll run to the ends of the earth to help you get there."

I buried my face in my father's shoulder. His embrace was solid and strong, and I wished it would go on forever. When I finally looked up, I saw that Lee had tears in his eyes. My mom stepped forward to give me a big hug also, and then they both left, so that Lee and I could talk in private.

He and I sat in the living room and talked and cried together. We both knew it was over. I could see that Lee was terribly hurt and angry. And there was nothing I could do or say to change things. The hardest thing I ever had to do was to walk out of the room knowing that Lee and I would never be together again. I felt as though someone had ripped my heart right out of my chest.

In our five years together, I had never had reason to question Lee's love, his faithfulness or loyalty. How had I repaid him? I stole from him to support my drug habit. I lied to him repeatedly. He gave me love and support; I gave him heartache and disappointment.

But I was an addict. I had lost control of my life. Crack was now in control and crack doesn't care about feelings or relationships. I gave up everything for crack. I spent thousands of dollars of my own money on crack and thousands of Lee's money, too. I lost my car, my home, my pets, and my job. I lost weight. I lost friends.

And finally, I lost one of the best men I have ever known.

Chapter 6
"In the Danger Zone"

Losing Lee was the end of my illusions. He was not only a wonderful man whom I had repaid with heartache, but he was also my last tenuous tie to a decent, happy, productive life. For several days, the crushing reality of it all was simply too much for me to process. I felt numb most of the time, tortured by the pain of the past and terrified by the prospects of facing life alone as a drug addict.

There were no dreams now, no fantasy world to escape to. I felt hopeless, powerless. I was convinced that I'd never be free from crack. I could not think of a single person I knew who smoked crack and was able to walk away from it for any length of time. It was impossible, I told myself, and realizing the futility of my situation, I quit caring, quit fighting, and quit hoping. All I really wanted to do was get high and forget. I didn't want to feel anymore and the only way I knew to accomplish this was to get high on a continual basis and that is exactly what I planned to do.

I didn't have a job or any money, so I spent most of my time roaming the streets, hoping to hustle up a high. That's how I ran into Tyrone. He made me a great deal: In exchange for a ride, he would give me dope and pay for gas. So I drove him and his cousin around as they sold crack around the 'hood. We drank and got high all night. We did it again the next day and the day

after that. We would crash at different houses or cheap hotels, wake up and get high all over again.

At some point during the binge, Tyrone told me that he had always liked me and looked up to me. This seemed odd to me. I was a failure, just another crack head. Funny, Tyrone would not be the only person who seemed to be drawn to me during my years as an addict. Years later, after I had gotten sober, I would run into some of my old running buddies who had also managed to escape addiction. The portrait they painted of me back then was far different than my view of myself.

"There was always something different about you," Clarence told me. "As bad as things were, no matter how dirty or strung out or hungry or desperate you were, there was always something decent about you, a spark. It's like you never lost that part of yourself, that good part of a person that gets lost when he or she is a drug addict."

"You were the only person I knew who said "please" and "thank you" to the dope man," said Tony, who was my partner in crime and would later re-emerge in my life in a most unexpected way. "Most of the people on the street, they're like dead people. You see it in their eyes - just a blank stare. But you were alive. Even in the worst times, you were always fun and people were drawn to that. I know I was," said Tony.

The idea that I was anything but an addict without hopes or dreams were something I was never able to see. People thought I was fun-loving, and I guess there was some reason for them to feel that way. But my life felt to me like it was a never-ending misery.

Tyrone not only liked and admired me; he also wanted us to be a couple. He said we could make a lot of money selling crack. That last part of the equation really appealed to me.

That meant I could get high without having to come up with my own hustle. Naturally I agreed to his proposition.

Tyrone was making good money as a drug dealer, so we went to get an apartment.

We went to buy some furniture and then headed for Brannan Homes housing projects to buy food stamps from some of the crack heads. Once we had set up house-keeping in the apartment, we sat around all day, every day, drinking, smoking weed and crack, and driving around the city to sell drugs. We sold directly out of my car most of the time, but we would also set up shop at convenience stores and gas stations in the 'hood. The only place we didn't sell from was the apartment. We didn't want customers or cops showing up on our doorstep.

It wasn't necessarily a cash business. We got jewelry, cars and clothes as payment, too. When the crack supply ran low, Tyrone and I would drive down to Phoenix to buy more drugs from the Mexican dealers on the west side of town or from the homies down on Buckeye Road and the Jamaicans on 24th street and Broadway on the south side.

Most of the time, we would buy the crack in rock form, although occasionally we got the drug in powder form. When we got back to Flagstaff, we would cut the block in $10 and $20 rocks and start the selling process again.

In the dope game, there is always the fear of getting caught or using more of your product than you sell. Soon, I began to want more crack than Tyrone was willing to give me. We were not equal partners; I resented not being able to smoke as often and as much as I wanted to. That led a lot of arguments and fights, naturally.

My split with Tyrone came without any premeditation. One day when Tyrone was supposed to meet a guy about buying a car, he sent me on an errand. Because male police officers were reluctant to search females, I always carried the dope. So I had his dope with me when I went out on the errand. I don't remember exactly where it was I was supposed to go or what I was supposed to do. All I know is that I went directly to a friend's house and proceeded to smoke all of the crack I had on me.

I don't know how long I was there, but it was long enough for Tyrone to become suspicious. He finally tracked me down at my friend's house and took my keys from me. He returned a little while later with all of my stuff.

After that, I moved back and forth between my friends' houses and my parents' home. But being back at home with my parents was very uncomfortable. There was tension in the air when just my mother and I were in the house, and so I just used their house as a place of storage for my belongings, a hot shower, a meal, and a quick nap. I really felt my situation was humiliating, and that made it even worse. Seeing me in that condition was heart-breaking for my parents, though, so I spent as little time at their home as possible.

Oddly enough, finding a place to stay wasn't really my first priority. Getting high was always the most important thing in my life at any given moment.

Crack is often portrayed as the poor man's drug of choice. Even so, a serious crack addict can spend hundreds or even thousands of dollars a day on drugs. And that money has to come from somewhere. For many, it comes from crime – robbing, stealing, prostitution, etc.

But I found another way to feed my habit, using the very thing that had once alienated me from the black community--my ability to interact comfortably with white people. This quality proved to be the basis for my first hustle.

I fell in with another group of small-time dealers in Flagstaff. We would rent a couple of hotel rooms in town, and I'd scout out the potential marks, usually white men or women looking to get high.

Basically, I was the runner. I would go to the mark's room, get his money and then go down the hall to where my partners were held up to buy drugs, always keeping a little of the cash and a little of the dope for my own use. You might say I was a retailer in what is usually a wholesale business.

It turned out to be a pretty good arrangement all around, but my associates had greater ambitions. The leader of the group was Herman, a young black man from Phoenix. There were three or four other young black men in the group, all from Phoenix.

In the spring of '92, Herman and the boys had shared with me their scheme that would finance their drug business. The plan involved going to Phoenix and pulling off some credit card scams. I was not a committed member of the group. My main interest in them was the supply of crack they always seemed to have.

When Herman asked me if I wanted to go to Phoenix with them to run the scam, I said sure.

I never did know much about the plan, how it worked, or what my role would be. All I knew is that there was a good chance I'd be able to get high. That was all I really needed to know.

We left Flagstaff for the three-hour drive to Phoenix in May. We were supposed to stay just a week or so.

We spent the first few days in Phoenix staying in cheap hotels on Van Buren St., an area notorious for drugs and prostitution. Somehow, the credit card scam fizzled out – again, I'm not sure of the details. After about a week or so, we wound up in an area on the city's south side known as "The Vistas," a neighborhood of small, closely crowded houses of five or six streets laid out in a U shaped pattern. The Vistas had one of the most notorious gang neighborhoods in Phoenix at a time when the gang and crack cocaine problem had reached its most dangerous stage.

A couple of the guys in the Flagstaff group lived in the neighborhood, so they knew their way around. We stopped first at a woman's house that was used as a place to cook, cut and package crack. I had never seen a brick-sized block of crack before and my first thought was that I would have a heart attack if I smoked that much crack.

I was so amazed by what I was seeing that I hardly noticed that the woman had a couple of small children running around in the house, which had no electricity. Now, I think about what a horrible life those children had. At that moment, though, all I was thinking about was smoking as much of that brick as they'd let me have.

It was that insatiable appetite for drugs that muted any natural fears I might have had. I was surrounded by strangers with guns and money and drugs. Yet I never once feared for my safety. I never gave it much thought.

The enduring memory of my first experience with a drive-by shooting, was me hitting the floor while still trying to smoke my crack pipe as the pop, pop, pop of the bullets tore through the drywall and sent glass flying around the room and the smell of gun powder hung in the air like a fog.

Virtually every night, the neighborhood would echo with gun shots. You never saw a single patrol car in the neighborhood, either. The police came in units of two or three cars, as a safety precaution. I remember an experience I had months later, after being picked up for questioning, a patrol car

stopped in the Vistas to put me out. I wouldn't get out of the car, for the fear of being labeled a snitch. Virtually every house in the neighborhood was home to a drug dealer or gang member and surely, someone would see me. I refused to risk being seen getting out of that patrol car in that neighborhood, even if it meant going to jail. And I didn't. The cop dropped me off about a half-mile away from the neighborhood and I walked back.

The Vistas was a Bloods neighborhood and their color was red. A few blocks away fell under control of the Crips, where the color was blue. I never understood the whole gang mentality; it was completely foreign to everything I had known. It struck me as not illogical: people willing to kill or die to control an area they didn't even own. It made no sense to me at all.

We had not been there more than a week or two. Later that same night, Herman and the boys decided to go back to Flagstaff, so I had a decision to make. I gave it careful thought. On one hand, I was an unaccompanied woman who didn't know a single person in the whole city, living among gang-bangers and drug dealers in one of the most dangerous neighborhoods in Phoenix.

On the other hand, these people had crack, and it was much more plentiful here than it was in Flagstaff. "I'm staying," I said. I never returned to live in my home town.

After the boys left for Flagstaff, I spent the next 24 hours floating from one stranger's house to another, smoking crack all the while. At some point, a girl found me at one of the houses and told me she had been sent to give me a message: Herman had been shot and killed in a shoot-out in Flagstaff. I didn't believe her at first, so I ran down to the street to the house where Herman's relatives lived. They told me it was true: another young black man killed over dope and money. I was stunned, but nobody else seemed too shaken by the event. Life seemed to be very cheap in the Vistas.

I often wonder how I managed to stay safe. Just about every home was occupied by a gang-banger or addict or a dealer. There were shoot-outs three or four times a week in the little neighborhood. Guns were everywhere.

I knew that I could only get high for free for so long. At some point, I was going to have to find a way to finance my habit. I began to get creative. Not long after I had arrived in the neighborhood, I managed to get a ride a mile or so down the road to the Rainbow Market on Broadway and 24th Street. Rainbow Market was one of those places where, at any given time, there are always more people in the parking lot than in the store itself. The parking lot was one of those places where you could always score some drugs, pick up a prostitute or buy stolen merchandise.

But my interest in the going to Rainbow Market was far more innocent: I wanted to get some chicken wings. As I was coming out of the store, I noticed an old white man sitting in his truck. He motioned for me to come over, so I did.

He asked if I wanted to party with him. In those days, the answer to that question was always YES! So I hopped into the truck with this man I had never met and we headed off downtown to a trashy motel off Van Buren. He had some crack and we started smoking.

After a while, he began to ask if I would look at some pictures he had with him.

"What kind of pictures?" I asked.

He told me they were nude photos of his girlfriend. Over the years, there have been many, many times when I would have done just about anything for some crack. But I NEVER entertained the thought of prostituting myself. And since any woman on the

76

streets is bound to find herself being propositioned, I learned very early on to be thinking of an exit strategy.

I figured the old man was mentioning the pictures as a prelude to asking for what he really wanted. But it finally dawned on me that he really did just want me to look at some naked photos of his 50-something girlfriend.

Now, I had not even the slightest interest in looking at nude snapshots of somebody's girlfriend and kept trying to tell him that. But he stayed after me, finally offering me $40 just to look at the photos.

$40. Well looking at pictures couldn't be that bad. I agreed to look at the photos if he would pay me the money up front. He agreed and handed me the cash. One by one, he pulled out a snapshot of the same naked woman and showed it to me.

I was amazed at how de-sensitized I had become in my short time in Phoenix. Seeing loaded guns laying all over the place hardly raised an eyebrow anymore. Hearing the pop of gunfire just down the street scarcely captured my attention. But there are some things that are strange no matter how wasted you are. And this was one of those things.

He would hand me a photo and watch my face as I looked at the image of this middle-aged naked woman. It was almost as if he wanted feedback. But what was I supposed to say? "Gee, I like the way she did her hair in this one!" or "I used to have a bedspread just like that!" or "Oh, I think this is my favorite one of all! You really should get it framed!"

He must have had a hundred pictures or more. Twenty minutes passed and I finally got to the last picture. I was relieved.

Then he asked me to give him oral sex.

"Can't we look at the pictures again?" I asked.

No. He wanted oral sex, he said.

I declined. He offered to pay me. Again, I said no.

He went to the bathroom and I half expected him to emerge with a gun or a knife. Instead, he just told me that he was leaving. He said that since he had already paid for the room for the night I could stay as long as I didn't tear up the place and was gone by checkout time.

I was much relieved when he left. I smoked the last of the crack he had left for me, and then decided to see if I could find a store. Although I was unfamiliar with the area, it was easy to find a convenience store. I bought a bottle of Mad Dog 20/20 in the store, and then scored a 16th of crack from a guy who was hanging around in the parking lot. I went back to the room and drank and smoked for the rest of the night. I went to sleep around 6 a.m. and the next thing I know it's 11 a.m. and the hotel manager is banging on the door telling me to get out.

I didn't know anybody in the area, so I was at a loss for where I would go. Then I remembered that I had George's number. George was an alcoholic who I had met during my first days in Phoenix. He seemed a little less threatening than most of the other men in the Vistas. He had a crush on me, and offered to let me live with him in the house he shared with his invalid mother and two brothers. I declined his generous offer at first, but had taken his phone number and kept it in my pocket. I called him and he said to take a taxi back to the Vistas and I could stay with him.

I stayed with George and his family off and on for the rest of my time in the Vistas. Mainly, though, I wandered the neighborhood, meeting people and getting high. I went back to George's place only when I wanted to crash and get some sleep in a safe place. In my moments of clarity I also went to church services at New Jerusalem Baptist Church, in South Phoenix.

There were a lot of people from Flagstaff there so I felt comfortable and at home there. On those days I would just pour my soul out to God, and hope for the best. I had very little faith left then. I knew in my heart that God was neither happy nor pleased with the choices I was making, but I wasn't able or even willing to let go of my addiction.

Even though the Vistas were a very dangerous place, I quickly learned who I could trust and who I should avoid. Among the local personalities were the Goudeaus, a large family of brothers and sisters. The name "Goudeau" became a household name in Phoenix when one of the brothers Mark Goudeau, was charged with 71 felony counts, including nine for murder, in the infamous "Baseline Killer" case.

I got to know some of the Goudeaus pretty well – Sonny, Peewee, Jake, Michael, and Richard.

I started hanging out with the Goudeau brothers and hooked up with Richard. Although I liked Richard, I was with him mainly because I thought he would keep me supplied with crack. He was a big talker, and at first I believed all of his stories.

Richard and I would get high almost every night. Early in the morning, he would leave, claiming that he had to go to work. He always left me wherever it was that we were. Often, we would wind up in houses with no electricity or plumbing. During the summer, the heat was almost unbearable and I found myself in a constant state of dehydration.

Many of the houses had been vacant for a while and were boarded up. Trash was everywhere and you had to be careful as you walked for fear of stepping on discarded needles or broken bottles. Used condoms and broken crack pipes littered each room and the odor was so bad you had to fight the reflex to vomit. People would use the toilet, even though it was broken.

Even worse, they would use the bathtub as a toilet. It was not uncommon to find a bathtub with three or four inches of standing urine and feces. There were easily the filthiest, most disgusting places I had ever been and yet I spent hours, sometimes days, in those houses getting high. I had been in Phoenix just three weeks and already I was acclimated to living like a wild animal.

The more I got to know the area, the more street wise I became. I soon caught on to Richard's compulsion to lie, distort and embellish. I finally confronted him about the lying one night when we were hanging out at Sonny's and he went sort of crazy, making all sorts of threats. I think he was trying to intimidate me, but by this time I was pretty much fearless. I had no life, no hope, very little to lose and even less to live for. It's hard to scare people when they get to that point.

After listening to his rant for a while, Sonny finally got tired of his antics and threw him out of the house. I stayed for a while drinking beer and then went to back to the Hubbards' to get some sleep.

At about 1 a.m. I woke up with the hunger to get high. I was walking down the street when Richard's brother, Michael, pulled up in his car and told me to get in. We rode over to Bell Road to pick up some dope and a friend of his who needed a ride. When we got back, Michael dropped me off at Sonny's house.

Richard was standing out in the front yard. Everything in the Vistas is cramped. The streets are narrow and the houses sit close to the street; about 20 feet from the front door to the street. So if you are standing the front yard of a house, you are only a few steps from the street.

Richard and I were facing the street as we talked; we were next to a couple of old palm trees that grew between the curb and the house. A big white car began to roll slowly down the

street in our direction. I noticed it out of the corner of my eye. As it approached, a shot rang out.

Richard grabbed me and took me to the ground. Just before my face hit the dirt, I looked up and saw three black faces with blue rags on their heads hanging out of the passenger side doors. They were shooting at us from basically point-blank range. Somehow, I managed to pull myself behind one palm tree as the bullets whizzed past me, kicking up furious clouds of dust. The shots echoed off the palm and I could feel the impact of the bullets against the tree trunk. The smell of gunpowder choked the night air.

I was in terror, but a strange calm came over me. I knew in my heart that if I made it through now, it was because God was watching over me keeping me alive. I began to see scenes from my past unfold, random bits of memories and experiences – myself sitting in a kindergarten class, the faces of relatives, my high school graduation.

The bullets continued to come in waves for what seemed like an eternity. In truth, it had been only a few seconds. Soon, people were pouring out of the house next door, firing at the white car, which sped off down the road in a shower of gunfire.

I was shaking all over. I managed to pull myself up into a sitting position against the palm tree and tried to catch my breath. I could feel my heart beating furiously in my chest as I gasped for air.

After a couple of minutes, I tried to stand but it was as if my left foot had fallen to sleep. I couldn't seem to move it. It didn't hurt at first. But I knew something was terribly wrong when I saw blood squirting out from the side of my boot.

Then the pain hit, the worst pain I'd ever felt. It felt as though someone was stabbing my foot with an ice pick on one side of my foot and burning me with a blow torch on the other.

I yelled out to Richard that I had been shot. He answered by saying he had been shot, too. I began to panic, afraid that the car was simply making the block and would soon be back to finish us off. I began to crawl, my foot oozing a bloody trail in the dirt behind me as I headed for Sonny's car. The plan was to hide under the car if the shooters came back around.

I looked up to find Sonny standing over me with this horrified look on his face. I stretched my hands toward him: "Oh, God. Sonny, I've been shot! Help me!"

Although drive-bys were not unusual in the Vistas, people did begin to congregate in front of the house out of mild curiosity. Someone yelled for somebody to call 911, and another person answered that an ambulance was already on the way. I asked a girl who was there to please call my brother Dwight, and let him know where I was and what had happened.

The gang-bangers in the neighborhood then began their interrogation. Who was it, they wanted to know. I told them I had never seen those people before, didn't know why they shot at us. Richard, who turned out to have only been slightly injured, began intimating that I was somehow to blame for the shooting.

Later, it turned out that the target had been Richard, but he tried to shift the focus on me to save his own hide, I figure.

My foot was still throbbing in pain, but I was suddenly desperately thirsty. Sonny ran to get me some water, but I couldn't seem to get enough. When the paramedics arrived, they refused to let me drink any more water because they said I was going to need surgery. I watched in horror as they took the boot off my foot. The blood continued to pour out of what used to be my ankle.

They put Richard and me in the same ambulance for the ride to the hospital and Richard talked the whole way. If I had been able, I would have gotten off that stretcher and strangled him.

When we arrived at the hospital, my stretcher was pushed up against a wall as I waited for an examination room to open up. I was screaming in pain by now. When I was at last taken into the examination room, I was beginning to fade. I heard the doctors and nurses talking about MRIs and X-Rays and surgery. The main doctor walked away and pulled a curtain behind him. But I overhead him tell someone that it seemed likely that there could be an amputation. I looked at my foot and began to cry. I begged the nurses not to let anyone cut off my foot. They tried to reassure me.

A surgeon came to examine me and told me he was pretty sure that he could save my foot, although he didn't know how much use I'd be able to get out of it.

As he wheeled me toward the operating room, I was beginning to drift off. I realized that when I woke up there was a very good chance I'd be a cripple – a homeless, addicted cripple at that. On the bright side, maybe I wouldn't wake up at all.

Chapter 7
"Living on the Streets"

I awoke from surgery to find my mother and father, Dwight and Sharon, and a few friends from home and from New Jerusalem Baptist Church gathered round me. Seeing those familiar faces made me feel, at least for a few moments, as if I had simply awakened from a nightmare.

But as I got my bearings, I realized that I had not been dreaming. I looked down at my bandaged foot. My leg was a mass of swollen flesh up to my knee. I found out later that I had been shot with a .357 magnum and possibly also a 9 mm. The bullet or bullets did such damage that it was impossible to determine how many times I had been shot.

My sister friend, Karen, was with me when the nurses came to dress the wound. When the bandages were removed, I was horrified. There was a gaping hole where my ankle had once been. The bones were shattered by the impact of the bullets to the point that my entire ankle joint had to be removed. I could see exposed muscle and tendon and the jagged edges of the bones that had been shattered. The pain began to come again as they cleaned the wound. Karen held me as I sobbed uncontrollably.

Despite the assurances of the doctors and nurses, I began to doubt if I'd ever be able to walk again. My foot looked horribly deformed. I couldn't imagine ever being able to use it. At first, the nurses gave me morphine for the pain, but later put me on

Demerol. A few days later, I was fitted with a cast that had an opening in it so that the wound could be packed with bandages soaked in a saline solution and medicine until I could have plastic surgery.

In the meantime, I went to physical therapy to learn how to get around on crutches, a wheelchair and a walker. I was told as soon as I learned how to get around I'd be released from the hospital.

Richard visited only once during my hospital stay. He had been shot through his calf, but the bullet did little damage.

He had learned some more details about the shooting. We weren't the only casualties, as it turned out. One of the shooters from the drive by had been killed; another was recovering from a gunshot wound just a few doors down from my room.

Again, Richard tried to fix the blame on me for the shooting, but I wasn't buying it. I had not done anything that would make me a target, I told him. I hadn't ripped off a dealer or sold fake dope to anyone. I pointed out that he, on the other hand, was a notorious liar. I was pretty sure Richard had a lot more to do with the shooting than he was willing to admit. All I know is that as soon as I turned the focus on him, he suddenly didn't want to discuss the shooting any more.

I had called George a few days after I arrived in the hospital and he told me I could stay at his house when I was released. His sister picked me up and took me to get my pain med prescriptions filled. The Hubbards' had fixed up a place for me in a back room, but I wasn't able to get comfortable. The pain began to hit me in waves and the pain meds did little to soothe me.

George's sister took me back to the hospital just a few hours after I had been discharged and the doctors put me on morphine, and a few muscle relaxers. Then they gave me prescriptions for stronger pain meds, and released me.

I spent the next few days in the back room of the Hubbards' house, popping pain pills, drinking, smoking weed and crack.

I was able to mend fences with the Goudeau clan after convincing them that I had not been the target in the drive-by. Richard and I were finished, of course, but I still needed to hang on to the few friends I had in the Vistas. Friendless people don't last long in that neighborhood.

Adding pain meds to my regular intake of alcohol, weed and crack left me in an almost constant high condition. Although pain pills weren't my drug of choice, they proved useful. I was able to sell pills or exchange them for crack.

I was in and out of the hospital for surgery, going right back on the street to get high each time. Eventually, my foot had healed to the point where I could get a skin graft, but it took four attempts for the skin graft to take. I suspect the unsuccessful grafts may have been due to my almost constant drug abuse during that time. Even with the skin grafts, my foot was a pretty sorry sight.

The bigger issue, though, was my mobility. I became pretty adept at getting around on crutches and I became a familiar figure hobbling back and forth between the dope houses, where crack was purchased, to the crack house, where it was smoked.

I abandoned the crutches as soon as I could, even though it was very painful to walk. This was not a matter of vanity. I knew that in the Vistas, a woman on crutches draws a lot of attention – all of it unwanted.

There were people in that neighborhood that saw a person on crutches as an easy target. The best defense any woman living in that environment has is the ability to run, to escape. A person on crutches is an easy mark for a would-be gang-banger who needs to notch a shooting to be initiated into the gang. Rapists also find a woman on crutches as an attractive target.

So I limped around as best I could. It was a matter of survival.

One day, as I was limping off to score some crack, I was especially loaded. I had taken some pain pills, chased them with some Thunderbird wine mixed with grape drink and had smoked some weed and some crack. I ran out of the crack, though, so it was off to the dope man to get some more. The dope man was selling crack out of an ice-cream truck parked in his yard. I bought some crack and as I was leaving, I heard George and Willie yelling at me to watch out.

But I was so high I could hardly see. I thought George and Willie were just trying to get my attention, that they wanted some of my dope. So I ignored them.

A moment later, I felt the impact of the car. George and Willie had tried to warn me that a car was backing out of a driveway where I stood. The blow knocked me into the street, but as high as I was, I clutched my dope, crack pipe and wine like a mother hen would shelter her chicks. I didn't lose a crumb of my dope or a drop of my wine.

I was so high that being hit by the car didn't even hurt. I picked myself up, gathered my stuff and proceeded to the crack house.

The next day, I managed to get a ride to Rainbow Market, where I was hanging out in the parking lot, getting high and eating chicken wings. A pimp in green Cadillac drove up to the take-out window of the Chinese restaurant next to the market. He had one of his girls in the car and when the food was ready, he told the girl to share the food with another girl who was standing near the drive-through window.

The pimp pulled over and parked his car and began to talk with a few men who were hanging around.

I didn't know any of the people involved, and wasn't really paying too much attention to them. The two girls began to argue loudly and I watched as they began to fight. One of the girls picked up a bottle, broke it on the curb and began chasing the other girl all around the parking lot. The pimp and other men thought it was hilarious. The girl who was being chased ran past me. Just as I was turning to see if the other girl was still chasing her, I felt a stinging pain in my back. The other girl had shoved the jagged bottle into my back, for a reason I guess I'll never know.

I screamed in pain as the glass went into my skin and screamed some more as she pulled the bottle out. I was bleeding profusely as the pimp performed his own peculiar method of first aid, which began and ended with wrapping a plastic garbage bag around me. He put me in the car, drove me to the hospital emergency room and then sped off.

A few hours later, I was back in the Vistas, with even more pain meds. I was seeing two doctors and a plastic surgeon at the time and had prescriptions from all of them.

I don't think a human being has ever been as high as I was over the next few weeks. Every waking hour I was using some sort of drug. And despite the stupefied condition I was always in, I never turned down a chance to get more crack.

One of those opportunities presented itself when Michael happened by and asked me if I wanted to go to a dope house off of Broadway where he had a "job" as the doorman. The dope house was located in a little apartment, which had almost no furniture in it. It was, as they say, functional. The apartment was used almost exclusively as a place to buy and smoke crack or have sex with a strawberry. A strawberry is a woman who will engage in any type of sexual act for drugs. Michael got some crack from the dope man and we went off to one of the empty bedrooms to smoke. He was in and out, answering the door, running down to the store to buy alcohol or cigarettes, that sort of thing.

Michael and I were back in the room getting high when the dope man called Michael into another room. Michael came back and told me that the dope man would give me two $20 rocks in exchange for sex.

Michael told me that this guy was not someone I could play around with. "He's very serious about his money and his dope," he said. "If you're not planning on having sex with him, you had better not take his dope. You better just leave if you're not going to have sex with him. That would be the safest thing."

I had no reason to doubt what Michael was saying. But, still, I wanted to get high and I was hoping I could talk my way out of the situation and still get some crack. I had done this before, plenty of times, in fact.

"Go get me some dope," I said.

"Are you sure?" Michael asked. "You're not going to have sex with him, are you?"

"No," I said. "Just cover for me after we get high and help me get out of the house. I'll handle the rest."

Michael reluctantly agreed.

He returned with the dope and we smoked all of it.

The dope man came in a little later and told Michael to leave.

"Take off your clothes and get on the bed," he said.

I tried to fumble for words, looking for a way out of the situation.

"I told you to take off your clothes," he said, his voice rising.

I tried to stall. I told him that if he would let me leave, I'd go down the street, get some money and bring it to him.

He didn't want money, he said.

I offered him the Demerol pills I had with me.

He didn't want that, either.

He started to scream and curse at me, telling me I wasn't leaving the room without paying him, one way or another. Well, really, he was in the mood to accept only one method of payment and I wasn't about to do that. He tried to push me onto the bed, but I fought back, which made him even angrier.

He flew into an absolute rage. Grabbing a piece of water hose, he began beating me. I tried to cover my face and screamed for Michael, but when Michael opened the door, the dope man chased him out.

He then began to pound on me with his fists. He spat on me, called me every filthy name he could think of. I tried to get away, and managed to crawl toward the closet.

The dope man got real quiet for a moment. I hoped that the violence was over. Then he lit a blunt – a cigar stuffed with weed.

"I'm going to teach you a lesson about smoking dope and not paying for it," he said. He came over the corner I was crouched in, grabbed my hair and began dragging me across the room. He pulled my left arm away from my face and began pushing the searing red-hot blunt onto my forearm.

I was screaming from fear and pain and terror as I saw and smelled my flesh burning. He lost his grip on me briefly and I flew toward the window, hoping to jump out even though the apartment was on the second floor of the building. I didn't know if I could survive the fall, but I knew that if I stayed in the room, this man was going to kill me.

Michael started banging on the door, screaming that the police were on the way. The dope man believed him, apparently. He left the room and Michael came in and helped me to my feet.

I managed to stumble out of the apartment, down the stairwell and into the street, hobbling along on one good leg, my body convulsing with shakes from the trauma of what had just unfolded.

A woman in a truck was driving by just as I staggered out on the sidewalk and gave me a ride to the Hubbards', where George applied ice to my burns and welts.

I took a shower, swallowed a handful of pain pills and finally got some sleep.

During my few months in the Vistas, I had been shot, hit by a car and stabbed with a broken bottle by a crazy prostitute and beaten and burned by an enraged dope dealer.

You might think that all of those experiences might have caused me to take a personal inventory and make some decisions about whether living in the Vistas was a good idea.

But when you are crack head, you don't make decisions. You make choices.

Believe me, there's a difference.

It would be a long time before I made any decisions.

Until then, I just made choices.

And almost all of them were bad ones.

After I recovered, I continued to pop pills, drink, and smoke weed and crack as though nothing had ever happened. A few days after the beating, I went to one of the housing projects to get high with some people I knew and we eventually ended up on Buckeye Road at an apartment of a guy named Don. Don and I sort of hit it off almost immediately and I soon came to see him as sort of a big brother. I got high with Don for a few days, smoking crack and giving him some of my pain pills.

Don was a few years older than me and was on disability. His disability checks kept a roof over his head. He couldn't work, so really his main focus was smoking crack. Don introduced me to some of the people in the neighborhood and I soon found myself surrounded by a new group of friends. Although Don and I never really discussed it, I sort of moved into Don's apartment. My new friends would come over to get high with me. It worked out to Don's benefit, too. It was sort of an unwritten rule. If you came to Don's house to party with me, you had to share your dope with him.

Don and I had a lot of fun together. We'd watch TV and play dice and card games. But mostly, we smoked crack.

More and more people began showing up to get high with us. One of those guys was a guy named Keith and it was Keith who really was the driving force in my permanent departure from the Vistas. Before I met Keith, I figured I would eventually wind up back at the Vistas since I never considered my situation at Don's place as anything permanent.

In many ways, Keith was not much different than any of the other men I met during my drug days. But he did have one quality that set him apart.

If lying or being a liar had been an Olympic sport, I'd have to say that Richard would have been on the podium for the awards ceremony. But they would be hanging the gold medal around Keith's neck.

I have never met a man who had a greater passion for lying than Keith. I swear, I think there were times when Keith would lie simply for the pleasure it gave him. He would lie even when telling the truth would have served his purpose better. By the time we parted ways, I was convinced that lying had been such a big part of his identity that he could hardly distinguish between truth and falsehood.

93

By this time, I scarcely resembled the naïve little girl from Flagstaff. The hard knocks I had absorbed during my time in Phoenix and my association with Richard, himself a liar of the highest order, had left me pretty street-wise.

One day Keith showed up at Don's apartment with a young white guy named Daniel, who Keith had just met at the dope house. Keith said they were going to go to the store and cash Daniel's paycheck, which meant there were two things unusual about Daniel: He was white and he had a job. Both were oddities in this part of town.

As bad as my association with Keith would turn out to be, it was even worse for Daniel.

As Keith and Daniel were leaving Don's apartment to cash the paycheck, Keith asked me if I wanted to tag along. He said they were going to cash the check, then buy some dope. That last part caught my attention.

"Sure," I said. A short while later, I'd be introduced to an area of town called "The Zone" which a dozen or so city blocks near downtown Phoenix that would soon become my "home," for lack of a better term.

Van Buren Street is infamous throughout Arizona as ground zero in the drug and prostitution trade. It is also the major thoroughfare through The Zone.

After cashing the check, Keith, Daniel and I wound up at the Desert Inn, known on the streets as "The D. I." The D.I. was a cheap hotel located across the street from University Park. University Park was sort of the Day Center of the homeless, a place where people could hang out and get high without being hassled much by the police. The police, quite frankly, had sort of given up on the area or at least it seemed.

We got a room at the D.I., then headed out to buy new crack pipes, screens, lighters cigarettes and wine – the crack addict's

version of setting up housekeeping – and then proceeded to get high and stay high.

Already, Keith had decided that he and I were going to be a couple. He told Daniel that he would have to sleep in his truck. Daniel meekly complied. He didn't argue; he just got up and went out to the truck. Keith and I continued to get high, drink wine and smoke cigarettes. Every now and then, Daniel would come back to get more crack. When the crack was gone, we spent the rest of the night roaming the streets, buying crack and getting high. Keith would put a whole $20 rock on my pipe for me to smoke, but he was not so generous with Daniel. He would give Daniel $20 work of crack while Keith and I held on to about $300 worth.

Mind you, all of the crack came from Daniel's paycheck. The poor sap. He never did catch on.

As long as Daniel had a paycheck, Keith and I stayed loaded. At one point, I smoked so much crack that I felt as if I was suffering a heart attack. Keith put me in a cold shower, gave me wine to drink and weed to smoke, all in an effort to lower my heart-rate. My heart was beating so fast that I was scared enough to stop smoking crack for a few hours.

After I felt a little better, we left the D.I. and went to Daniel's mobile home just south of Baseline Drive. Daniel, I realized, had all the qualities a crack addict looks for in a friend: He had a job and a home.

We hung out at Daniel's place for a few weeks, with Daniel going to work in the morning and Keith and I laying around getting high on his income. Daniel had recently been divorced and the wife and kids had moved out. But some of his wife's things were still in the mobile home, so while Daniel was at work Keith and I went through his closets for clothes we could wear.

As Daniel's slide into addiction began to pick up pace – hurried along, no doubt, with the help of his two new "friends" - he started missing work. Eventually, he was fired. Losing the job was a terrible blow – for Keith.

Without the income, there was the important matter as to how Daniel would keep Keith and me in the manner to which we had grown accustomed. Being the sort of stand-up guy that he was, Keith found a solution to this perplexing problem: he started selling off Daniel's stuff.

First it was the appliances. Then it was just about anything with arm's reach. After cleaning out the mobile home, Keith and Daniel used Daniel's truck to steal appliances and fixtures from vacant homes, rental properties and houses under construction.

I didn't go along on any of these capers, but I was more than happy to smoke the crack we bought from the sale of those things.

Sadly, all good things must come to an end. Keith and Daniel's friendship ended soon after Keith took Daniel's last remaining possession – his truck – and sold it to a Mexican drug dealer. The dealer took the truck down to Mexico, so Daniel had no chance to recover it.

They parted company in short order. I'd like to think that Daniel finally got wise. But, given his meek acceptance of everything Keith had done, I suspect that it was Keith who ended things. Daniel wasn't of much use anymore.

With the demise of the "Three Cracketeers," Keith and I faced the unpleasant reality of hustling up our own dope. For a while, we lived off the money Keith had made from the sale of Daniel's truck.

When that money was gone, Keith turned to breaking into businesses to steal whatever he could find. There was a Mexican

lady who had a booth at a swap mart and she would buy the stolen property from Keith and resell it from her booth.

I tagged along with Keith a few times, always reluctantly.

It was only a matter of time before his luck ran out. Finally, the police caught him selling stolen appliances out of a stolen rental truck to the Mexican lady. I happened to be just around the corner when the arrest happened and I managed to see the cops putting Keith in handcuffs and putting him in the squad car.

Goodbye, Keith, I thought. *Now what?*

I was in the park, surrounded by people I didn't know very well. I was scared. I didn't know how I was going to take care of myself. I didn't know where the shelters were, where you could get food, or clothes. I didn't have any money. Worse still, I didn't have any dope.

I sat in the park all night, keeping to myself and trying not to get noticed. It was a situation that had to change. And quickly.

Again, I was pretty much alone, but I wasn't afraid like I had been when I first arrived in the Zone.

As the months passed, I became more and more confident in my ability to survive on the streets alone. I had a lot of friends to protect me and I had become pretty street savvy, too.

But a friend isn't a companion. I was alone a lot of the time and the odds have a way of catching up with you.

I heard somewhere that there is a practical reason that zebras have stripes. It helps keep them alive. Lions, when stalking a herd of zebras, have a hard time telling where one zebra ends and another begins which gives the zebras a chance of survival when a lion makes its pounce. Often, the lion will miss his aim in the maddening confusion of a sea of black-and-white stripes. I wonder sometimes if a lion doesn't just throw up his paws and say, "Forget this! Let's go find some wildebeests. At least we can make heads or tails out of 'em."

But here is the other thing: The pattern only provides safety if the zebra is in a herd. A solitary zebra, with its bold black-and-white stripes, is about the most conspicuous thing in the savannah.

So I was sort of a solitary zebra on the streets. And the lions eventually took notice.

One night as I was walking through the streets, I decided to take a short-cut through an alley to the dope house. I had been on the streets for a couple of years by this time, so I knew the Zone inside and out, not only the streets but the alleys. I knew where all the dope dealers operated and the location of all the crack houses.

This night, I was really desperate to get high, so I decided to cut through an alley that I had always known, mostly by instinct, that I shouldn't go down. There wasn't really anything to distinguish this alley from the "safe" alleys. All of the streetlights had been knocked out or shot out, so it was pitch black. But even that didn't distinguish this alley from the others. All of the streetlights in the zone had been knocked out for years.

Against my better judgment, I headed through the alley anyway. About halfway through, I felt myself being knocked to the ground. I hit the ground in a cloud of dust and before I could react a man was tearing my clothes away, shoving himself between my legs.

It was over in what seemed like an instant, an attack so fast, so violent that it seemed to have ended before I could even figure out what was happening. Suddenly, the man was gone and I was lying there in the alley, covered in dust and my attacker's sweat.

I had been raped for the first time. I got up and continued down the alley to the dope house.

"I really need to get high," I told the dope man.

That was not only my form of rape counseling – get high and stay high and maybe you can forget – it was my solution to everything in my life at that point.

But you can't forget rape. You can only stuff it down somewhere inside you. It never goes away. It eats at you. You die from the inside out.

The rape did nothing to change my routine, really. I picked back up where I left off, still hustling to get high. It was the only focus I had in my life.

One day I was sitting in a car with a man who paid me $40 to watch him masturbate. I hated this part of the business, the sick, twisted perversions that came with making a buck. But $40 is $40. I was hungry and craving dope, so I watched this man do his thing. He paid me the $40, bought me some wine and cigarettes and dropped me off on 15th Avenue and Polk.

As I stepped onto the curb, a prostitute who everybody knew as "Psycho" approached me and asked me if I wanted to go get high with her.

So off we headed to a house that she often used to turn her tricks. She gave the man who owned the house some dope as payment and we went into a back room and starting drinking and smoking crack.

"Why are you hanging in the streets when you could be laying up in a room somewhere?" she asked.

"I'm not like you Psycho," I said. "I don't mean anything by that. It's just that I could never bring myself to work the streets, you know? It's just not my hustle."

Psycho didn't seem upset.

"I get it," she said, pausing a moment before she spoke again.

"Can I tell you something?" she asked.

"Sure," I said.

"Well, I've always had kind of a crush on you," she said. "If you would be my girlfriend, I'd take good care of you. You wouldn't have to live out on the streets. It would be great."

I fumbled for words.

"I know it seems strange and all. I only use men to get money. I love women," she said.

"Look," I said. "I'm not gay and I'm not going to put myself out on the streets, you know?"

"You don't have to do anything," Psycho said. "All you have to do is be my girlfriend. I'll take care of the rest. I'll take good care of you."

I began to turn it over in my mind. The idea of having sex with a woman was something that I had never thought about. I had never had even the faintest attraction to women.

But I thought of the life I had been living – homeless all the time, hungry most of the time, putting myself in one dangerous situation after another to get high.

And an addict always puts her own interests first in any relationship.

Maybe this wouldn't be so bad, I thought.

"OK," I said.

Looking back, Psycho and I did have a physical and emotional relationship. There is simply no denying it. I think we had both suffered so much abuse, that we desperately needed some kind of caring, comforting relationship. Sex was a very small part of our relationship, but it was a part of it.

But more than that, we were drawn to each other for many of same reasons you find in any relationship. For that period of time, Psycho played a significant role in my homeless journey.

Psycho took care of me. She tried to keep me safe. We were zebras together.

It worked well for a while. Psycho provided me with access to crack, and we offered each other some protection and affection.

But the situation deteriorated fast. Before long, I was going with Psycho as she turned her tricks, lying right beside her on the bed of some cheap motel or dope house as she had sex with men. I would get high as she and her trick went at it. I was completely desensitized. It didn't create any sort of emotional response at all.

I felt invisible, really.

It didn't matter. The only thing that mattered to me at that point was getting high. And being safe mattered, but it was secondary.

One day Psycho and I were getting high with one of her tricks, a guy named Leonard, at our hotel room. A knock sounded at the door. It was Cupcake Mike, a friend, there to tell Psycho that a trick was looking for a girl just down the street. Psycho told me to wait in the room while she went to pick up the trick, so Leonard and I stayed in the room and continued to smoke crack.

For some reason, Psycho didn't return right away – I figured the trick had picked out his own location to complete the transaction. When Leonard and I had smoked all the crack we had, he pushed me down onto the bed. I was stunned at first; one moment we were getting along fine, smoking crack, laughing and talking. The next minute, he was trying to force himself on me. I fought him off as best I could, but when I felt the point of a knife at my throat, my body went numb.

He threw me on the bed and raped me at knife point.

When he was finished, he got off me and said he was sorry. He started telling me that we should be a couple, that we could make a lot of money as a team. In so many words, he was trying to pimp me out.

I was stunned. The man who had just raped me at knife point was talking about being a couple and turning me out on the streets as a prostitute. My eyes went to the dresser, where he had laid the knife.

I could kill him. I thought.

I tried to put that thought out of my head. It frightened me even to think it. So I forced a smile and began to think how I could get away from Leonard.

He asked me if I wanted to take a shower with him.

"No," I said. "You go ahead."

At first, I thought I'd run out of the room as soon as he was in the shower. But the rage began to boil up inside of me. Somehow, I thought, he was going to pay for what he had done to me.

"You know what, let me take a shower first," I said, hoping that I could clear my mind and think of what to do next.

I went into the bathroom, locked the door behind me and stepped into the shower. Suddenly, I lost it. I began to sob uncontrollably, my body shaking with equal parts rage and emotional pain. I spent a long time in the shower, scrubbing my skin so hard I feared I'd bleed in a desperate, pathetic effort to rub away the feel of his body on top of mine. I was trying to erase the memories and the pain of my life. I wanted it to just wash down the drain.

I knew that Leonard had money; he had counted his money in the room earlier that day: $750.

When I managed to regain my composure, I came up with a plan to stab him and steal his money.

I wondered if Leonard would sense that I intended to do him violence, but when I got out of the shower, he seemed casual, as if nothing at all had happened. *You are a rat bastard.*

He got in the shower and I altered my plan. I just couldn't bring myself to pick up that knife and stab him. So I broke off the leg of a table in the room and slipped it under the bed.

Leonard came out of the shower, sat on the bed and began putting lotion on his body.

The time to act was now, I thought, but I couldn't summon up the courage. I went to the bathroom under the pretense of wanting to wash my hands. I was able to strengthen my resolve.

When I stepped out of the bathroom, Leonard was looking out the window, his back to me. "Perfect," I thought. "It's now or never,"

I reached under the bed to retrieve the table leg and in an instant; I had crossed the room and swung the table leg as hard as I could at his head. Leonard screamed in pain as I began to hit him on his head over and over until he finally sank to the floor, cowering.

I cannot say for sure what would have happened if my friend C Dog had not arrived at that moment. I might have beat Leonard to death. The rage inside me wasn't going away and with each blow of the table leg, I grew colder, angrier, and meaner.

But C Dog had heard the racket and burst through the door to grab me.

"What happened?" he asked.

I told him that Leonard had raped me at knife point.

C Dog began kicking Leonard, while he lay whimpering on the floor.

I saw Leonard's wad of money on the dresser, grabbed it and ran out of the room.

Just as I reached the sidewalk, I saw Psycho approaching.

"What?" she said alarmed at the condition I was in.

"Run!" I said as I sprinted down the sidewalk, not stopping to let her catch up.

She finally caught up with me on 7th Avenue. We walked to the Travel 9 Hotel on Van Buren without speaking. It wasn't until we were in the hotel room that I told her what had happened.

We went to the dope house for crack. We bought $200 worth of crack and went to the liquor store to buy wine, cigarettes and snacks. We stayed in that room getting high for days, leaving only to get more dope.

As I sat in that hotel room, I began to realize that I quit living a long time ago. I was just surviving, sort of like an animal, living solely by instinct and impulse. I didn't know who I was. I didn't know what mattered. I had quit caring about life, not just my own life, but life in general. I had beaten and robbed a man. He had raped me; he had it coming, I knew. But beating somebody with a table leg? Brenda Combs would never do that.

But I quit being Brenda Combs somewhere on the streets of the Zone a long time ago.

I kept smoking crack in that hotel room with Psycho. Until then, I had always been sure that crack could fix anything. You might need an awful lot of crack, but it could solve any problem, or at least make you forget it.

Well, we had more than enough crack to get the job done. Somehow, I thought, I just couldn't shake the darkness that had closed in around me.

I was sick. I was tired. I was so sad, so unhappy. But most of all, I was hurting inside. The pain was always there and no amount of crack could ease it.

I wanted to end the madness, to get off drugs and stay off drugs.

But I knew I couldn't. Not yet.

Chapter 8
You Can Lead an Addict to Rehab

When you are on the street, life can change dramatically and with dizzying speed.

One day, Psycho and I and a friend named Jimmy were cruising around town, getting high and having fun. The next thing I knew, I was sitting in the "Horseshoe," which is where suspects are held while being booked into jail.

I was particularly worried about finding myself in the Horseshoe, which was a wretched place. Its filthy, overcrowded cells with no beds, almost no supervision from staff, often had dangerous consequences when fights among inmates broke out. I'd already been there plenty of times, usually serving a couple of days or a week for some petty crime.

This time was different, though.

It turned out the car we were riding in had been reported stolen by its owner, Jimmy's girlfriend. Although I wasn't driving and wasn't charged with the theft, the officer did run my name through the system and found that I had outstanding warrants for probation violation.

Well, I had no argument. I had probably violated my probation a hundred different ways out on the street. I knew this time, I'd be "down" for a lot longer than a week.

I got 90 days in county jail, as it turned out.

In some respects, jail is a lot better than living on the streets. You can take a shower and you are provided a toothbrush and a

comb. Generally, your personal hygiene is a lot better in jail than out on the streets.

But freedom is precious and losing it makes jail pure hell.

Still, going to jail could have been a great opportunity to me. Removed from the maniacal, never-ending pursuit of crack, I could have had a chance to get sober, see myself with some clarity, and make changes.

I desperately wanted to get off crack and try to pick up the pieces of my shattered life. This was my chance.

Slowly, in bits and pieces, I began to reclaim small parts of my identity that had been lost in the years of living high and homeless on the streets.

One day as I was sitting in my pod playing cards, a tall white man came in. I noticed him out of the corner of my eye. He was going around, talking softly to the girls, sometimes praying with them.

The man made it over to where I was sitting and introduced himself to me. His name was Larry Sheer and he was a deacon at Christ Church Lutheran. He asked if I would join him in prayer. I agreed and after the prayer, we talked a while.

I told him that I grew up in Christian home and that I sang and played piano at my home church back in the day. He asked me if I would be interested in singing at the Lutheran services that were held at the jail each week.

Church services are very popular in jail, even among those who have no real interest in God or religion, because the services allow you to escape the monotony of living in the pod, even if it's only for an hour or so.

It had been a long time since I sang those hymns, but I have to admit that my singing was well received. In fact, a lot of the correction officers would listen at the door as I sang during the services. Deacon Sheer was able to get me special permission to sing at all of the jail's church services. This helped me a bit in the jail as the corrections officers treated me nicer, but its biggest impact for me was that it put me back in touch with God.

At that point in my life my faith was a fraction of what it had been before, but singing in services gave me the opportunity to ask God questions. I was very aware of my wretched state, even if I couldn't bring myself out of it. "Why is it taking so long for my change to come?" I would ask, and "Why do you even love me when I am such a disappointment to everyone?" I felt as if God was listening, which in itself was very healing.

While I was on the street, I always managed to stay in touch with my family on an infrequent basis. My brother and sister both lived in Phoenix. Both were hardworking, upstanding, and fairly independent. They were also very close. Dwight, who worked as a computer systems analyst in downtown, right down the street from the Zone, would sometimes drive around in hopes of finding me. When he succeeded, he would give me a few dollars or buy me a meal and try to assess how I was doing. Other times, he would find me but not try to talk to me. I think he realized that any help he offered me would be used only to feed my addiction. Still, he would look for me every now and then, just to make sure I was alive.

My parents would periodically come to Phoenix to visit Dwight and Sharon and go shopping. Sometimes they would look for me during those trips. I called my parents every few months, just to say hello and tell them that I loved them. Those conversations were short. My parents wanted me to come home, but they didn't want me to come home if I wasn't prepared to make some changes. I wasn't. They knew. I knew. Before long, the phone calls were pretty much limited to letting them know I was still alive.

During my 90 days, Dwight and Sharon came to visit a few times. But I couldn't handle their visits and asked them to stop. It tore me up to watch them walk out of that jail as free people while I was forced to stay behind. Again, you have to be a prisoner to understand that feeling.

So Deacon Sheer became my only visitor. He showed up every week, listening to me, encouraging me. He gave me his phone number and told me to call him when I got out of jail. Maybe there would be some way he could help me, he said.

As the days crawled by toward the end of my sentence, I became more and more determined to get my life back on track.

I had some help, too, in the form of my probation officer, a woman named Michelle Elbow. Unlike many of the P.O.s I had dealt with before, Michelle seemed to see me as a real person rather than just another case number that had to be dealt with. She would listen to me patiently as I talked about my life, my hopes and fears.

The value of having someone show a genuine interest in you cannot be overestimated. Michelle encouraged me and gave me hope that I could beat my addiction.

I went into Maverick House for a 45-day rehab, afraid but hopeful.

It was at Maverick House that I met my future husband, Jose Rodriguez. Since neither of us had visitors, we began to hang out together. Because of the nature of rehab, the relationships you make are often very intense. In that setting, you drop all pretenses. You share the most intimate, painful, horrible aspects of your life. You are completely vulnerable, which is a quality that you cannot permit yourself to exhibit out on the streets. For so long, I knew deep inside how vastly different my life was compared to how I was raised. I felt as though I was a freak and a loser. Meeting some else who had the same sort of emotional baggage created a powerful bond.

The counselors recognized what was happening between Jose and me. And they were not in favor of it.

I guess after you have been a drug counselor for a while, you develop a pretty keen sense of character. The counselors liked nothing about what they saw in Jose. I think they instantly recognized that there was little conviction behind his words. He said all the right things, but it was a guise, they were convinced.

They told me to put some distance between myself and Jose. They warned me that he was not going to be a positive influence in my life if my goal was to turn my life around.

But I didn't listen. I couldn't listen. Not then.

While Jose seemed to always say the right things, respond just the way you are supposed to in counseling sessions, I was generally viewed as someone who wasn't getting the message.

I suppose I can understand why the counselors and other residents might reach that conclusion. But I was through playing games. I was determined to be honest when talking about my feelings, my beliefs.

One day in a session, a counselor cited studies that showed that in a group of 100 people in a rehab program; only six would get sober and stay sober. The other 94 would have relapses, would probably wind up in jail and would eventually die as a result of their addiction.

Of course, Jose was absolutely convinced he would be one of the six who stayed clean. For my part, I hoped that I'd been one of those fortunate few, but wasn't entirely convinced. Nothing in my past suggested that kind of outcome, at least.

I wanted to get clean, but it was so much easier to get high. I was keenly aware of the strikes against me. My family hadn't given up on me, for which I was thankful. But everyone else was

very unforgiving. People from church, extended family, friends, and neighbors, would smile to my face but doubted that I could make it. Most people I knew were waiting for me to fail. One of my uncles told me that I was destroying the "Combs" name.

I wasn't convinced I'd be among the "Sober Six." I would pray to God about this, wondering why he saved me.

Jose, who had been the poster child for recovering addicts at Maverick House, was kicked out of the house under mysterious circumstances. He wound up at a halfway house called Steps House. A week after he left, I was kicked out of Maverick House for trying to have a letter smuggled to him.

I moved to Traditions, a co-ed facility, a week later and that is when my relationship with Jose really started.

Although I had been kicked out of Maverick House, I was still committed to beating my drug habit. But I can't say it was easy.

For one thing, I hated attending the mandatory Alcoholics Anonymous and Narcotics Anonymous meetings. For the most part, my impression of the meetings was that they were a waste of time. About the only thing I heard were addicts trading "war stores" of their addictions. It seemed to me very much like attending a high school reunion where everybody talks fondly of "the good old days." Well, I had my own stories, few of which I could recall with anything approaching fondness. I was looking for ways to cope with the cravings. I was looking for solutions and strategies. Instead, I got stories about getting high.

Aside from that, I got hung up on the first words that any addict is supposed to say at a meeting: "My name is Brenda and I am a recovering addict."

Saying those words always stuck in my throat. At that time, I had no interest at all in "recovering." The idea that I would spend the rest of my life in the process of recovering was too depressing

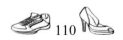

110

to consider. I wanted to be the other side of addiction, but what I heard in those introductions was a grim admission that I would never been on the other side of my addiction until I was on the other side of the grave. How sad, I thought.

If you have never had any experience with a halfway house, you might be inclined to think that they are safe places for addicts to go to fight their battle with drugs. But the truth is drugs and alcohol are everywhere you look at most halfway houses. Here's a hint, if you ever need to know where a particular halfway house is located, just ask a dope dealer. He'll know. Believe me, he'll know.

This was particular true of Traditions during the time I was there. The director, a woman purported to have 20 years of sobriety behind her, would go AWOL for days at a time, always returning with some sort of dubious excuse.

She was quick to kick people of the house, saying that they had failed drug tests, even though there were many occasions when her credibility could be questioned. It seemed like anyone she didn't like mysteriously failed a drug test almost immediately after a clash with her.

One day I returned from work and was informed by the director that all of the other girls had been kicked out of the house for having "dirty" UA's. She said I would have to take a drug test, too. That didn't worry me in the least. I had been living clean and had taken a drug test at my probation officer meeting earlier that day. It had come back "clean," so taking another test wasn't anything I was worried about.

I gave the director the sample. A short time later, she came back and told me to pack my bags and get out. I had tested positive for weed.

I was floored. I knew it was a lie. But what could I do?

I called my probation officer Michelle and told her what happened. I offered to take another test, but my probation officer said it wasn't necessary. She knew I was telling the truth. But I wanted to prove it. The probation officer came over and gave me a test. I passed, of course, as the director sat there in silence, never offering an apology.

I could have stayed, but I realized that the director would never stop until she found a reason to have me evicted. So I packed my things and moved to Oxford House for women.

A few weeks later, I heard that the director of Traditions had been found drunk and passed out in her office. She had also been taking some of the meds prescribed to the residents. Later, I found out that she had been arrested for DUI during my stay at Traditions. Clearly, I was fortunate to get out of there.

By this time, Jose was on intensive probation and seemed to be doing pretty well. Although we weren't supposed to have any contact, I did see him at the A.A. and N.A. meetings, so we were able to stay in touch. Soon, we found ways to be together at other times.

Jose was very kind and generous in those days. I was working a minimum-wage job, so I never had much of anything. Jose would give me money and buy me gifts. My dad had managed to get me a car so I could drive back and forth to work

So I was doing okay, I thought. I found precisely what I needed at Oxford House. I liked everything about the place. It was run entirely by the residents, who not only paid for all of the expenses but also had complete authority to establish and maintain the rules. What happened at the house was up to us. It felt good to be trusted with that kind of responsibility.

Residents elected officers, who served six-month terms. But the officers did not have complete autonomy. At any point, a person could be punished if a majority of the residents believed that any member had broken the rules. Anyone caught drinking or using drugs faced immediate expulsion. We had mandatory weekly meetings where we could discuss problems, offer suggestions and talk about house issues.

Because there was no paid staff, Oxford House was an affordable alternative to many other treatment centers. Residents were on their own to go to counseling or take advantage of a variety of programs at their disposal.

Oxford House was a beautiful four-bedroom house in North Phoenix and there were only eight residents during my time there. I shared the master bedroom with a former prostitute. I think the environment – a nice home in a clean, safe neighborhood – was of great value on a psychological level. Living there somehow gave me the feeling that I was stepping away from the filth and degradation that had marked my time on the streets. After living in that environment for a while, I began to feel as though I actually belonged there, and began to feel good about myself in terms of developing bonds and making friendships.

That is not to say that I was entirely free from my past. There were times when I would have flashbacks. There were moments when I would get in the shower and try to scrub away the memories. I knew that I wasn't free of those memories. I did not want the wreckage of my past to haunt my future. I found that by journaling and writing songs that expressed my feelings, the burden of those memories began to fall away. It was a big part of my life. It remains a big part of my life.

Sadly, not long after I moved into Oxford House, the lease expired and all of the residents were forced to move out. I found a cheap apartment in downtown Phoenix. My friend, Chuck, was also in a recovery program. He offered to help me move into my apartment. As we were moving in, I let him take my car so he could go to Jack in the Box get us something to eat. I stayed behind, organizing things in my apartment.

I was in the bathroom hanging up the shower curtain when Chuck returned. I walked out of the bathroom into a thick cloud of smoke I instantly recognized as crack cocaine.

Chuck hadn't gone for food, I realized. I didn't know that they sold crack at Jack in the Box!

There he was standing in my kitchen with this stupid grin on his face and a crack pipe in his hand.

Another crack pipe and a rock of crack cocaine were sitting on the kitchen counter.

I looked at the crack lying there on the counter and thought about it a minute or two. I thought about all the awful things that had happened to me as a result of crack cocaine. I thought of how much progress I had made, how hard it had been to get to the point where I was again living in a place of my own with a job and some hope for the future.

I thought of all that.

And then I picked up the pipe, loaded it with crack and began to smoke.

From that moment on, I began to plunge deeper into addiction.

In a matter of a few weeks, I left Jose, lost my job and my apartment, and was back on the street, back where I had been before my last-gasp effort to get clean.

Not much had changed. Oh, a few people I had known weren't around anymore. Some had gone to prison; some had gone to the cemetery. Everybody else, though, was pretty much were they had been when I left.

But I wasn't the same. I was worse. Much worse.

When you are out on the street, you usually have some faint hope that somehow you'll be able to turn your life around some day. But I had no delusions now. This was it, I told myself. Life would never again have meaning or hope or love.

I had an unshakeable feeling that I wouldn't live much longer anyway. And when you reach that conclusion, nothing matters. Do what you want and don't worry about the consequences. What are consequences when death lurks around the next corner?

For a while, I made some effort to hang on, but it was only a feeble attempt.

When I first hit the streets those long years before, I had a few possessions with me, mainly items of clothing that I pushed around in a stolen shopping cart. But when you're a crack addict, it's hard to keep up with stuff. It either gets stolen or you leave it behind as you wander off in a stupor from one crack house to another.

Sooner or later, I always wound up in a condition where the only clothes I owned were the clothes I was wearing.

On the streets, showers and baths are available only when you have enough money to get a hotel room. Sometimes weeks would go by before you had that kind of money and you can get so miserable living in your own filth that you will do almost anything to escape the grime.

Sometimes, I would go to the women's room at University Park in an effort to get clean. In those days, the soap dispenser was filled with the granulated, powder soap that had the consistency of laundry detergent.

I would take off my clothes and wash myself with the scratchy soap powder. I also used the powder to try to clean my clothes. If the sinks weren't working, I would put my clothes in the toilet, dump some soap powder in and swish my clothes around in the toilet. It was, quite literally, a crude form of a washing machine. I'd wring out my clothes as best I could and put them back on wet.

But sometimes even those pathetic attempts at hygiene were more than I could force myself to attempt. In the Zone, one of the popular gathering spots for the homeless was called the island which I refer to as Jurassic Park. It wasn't really a park at all, but a greenbelt that stretch about eight city blocks. Police have long since chased the homeless out of this greenbelt, but back then, people lived there not unlike animals. The grass was littered with human waste, but no one seemed to give it a thought.

Like all green areas here in the desert, the grass is kept alive through flood irrigation. And when Jurassic Park was flooded, I often rolled around in the filthy water to cool off. That all manner of filth, including feces, floated in the water never seemed to be a deterrent; I had grown accustomed to it.

When I returned to the streets, personal hygiene seemed to matter less and less and finally, not at all. My hair was matted and I had ants and bugs working through my scalp. I could feel a thick film on my teeth, gums and tongue, which is what, happens when you go weeks without brushing your teeth.

I was in a sorry state most of the time, but when I was on my menstrual cycle, I was nothing short of pathetic. I didn't have access to pads or tampons, so when I had my period I would use whatever I could find to stuff into my panties – if I had panties - to stem the flow. I would use wads of paper, cloth, anything I could find that could be fashioned into a crude pad.

Sometimes, I wouldn't even make that effort. I would simply bleed through my clothing and tie a plastic garbage bag around my waist to hide the blood.

When my period ended, I'd go down to Interfaith and get some clean clothes or hook up with some of the prostitutes and get clothes from them.

It has been said that humans have three basic needs: Food, clothing, shelter. But when you are crack addict, those needs are subjugated to a more pressing need: the need to get high.

That is why an addict will go days without eating, but can't last an hour without getting high. At rock bottom, I had probably dropped four dress sizes. That might sound impressive on some level, but believe me, this is a diet plan you do not want to pursue.

My appearance certainly would not have been something you would want to advertise. I had a gaunt, almost cadaver like physique. My eyes were dull, almost yellow and my skin had a dull luster, almost as if it were covered by some sort of murky film. My skin was dry and marked with welts, bruises and sores.

A homeless crack addict in her 30s looks much, much older. Soon, I became virtually unrecognizable. I remember one afternoon seeing a familiar car move slowly down the street. The car would pull up to a group of people and pause. Obviously, the person in the car was looking for someone.

I was standing at a street corner when the car pulled up next to me. The driver's eyes met mine. The light changed, and the driver crept forward, again stopping along the way, searching the faces of the people on the street.

The driver of the car obviously hadn't recognized me. But I recognized him.

It was my father.

As terrible as my physical condition had become, I can't say I was ever alarmed. My main focus remained on getting high. But I was often hungry, desperately hungry. Sometimes, I would

manage to make it to the Andre House or Vinny's at meal times. But more often than not, I missed out on those free meals.

On those occasions, I would go through the dumpsters at fast food places. At most of those places, there were rules about how long prepared food could be kept before it had to be thrown out, so I always kept a watchful eye for employees going to the dumpsters with garbage. If I was lucky, the expired food – usually burgers or chicken – would be placed in a separate garbage bag. Other times, the food would be dumped in with the rest of the trash before being carried out to the dumpsters.

In either case, I was not in a position to be choosy. The staff at those fast-food restaurants were under strict orders not to give food to homeless people because word of that would spread quickly among the desperate street people in the Zone. But the dumpsters were fair game and the only competition was the feral cats and rats that also depended on the dumpster for their sustenance.

Every so often, though, someone at a restaurant would take pity. One night I had managed to pull some chicken wings out of a dumpster. Unfortunately, the ants had discovered the chicken before I had, so I sat on the pavement next to the dumpster, brushing the ants off the chicken so that I could take a bite.

I was pretty focused on the task, so I never saw the cook of the restaurant as he approached me. I think he saw me out there on the curb, brushing ants off the garbage I was trying to eat.

As the ants and I were sharing the piece of chicken I happened to look up and see the cook standing in front of me. I was afraid he was going to tell me to leave, that he was coming to tell me that he had called the cops. Instead, he handed me a box of chicken, turned and walked away without a word.

But those sorts of kindnesses were rare. More often, life was just a tortured stagger into an endless night.

118

I will not say that I had become an animal by that point, mainly because it would be an unfair comparison – to the animals. Certainly, I had no more conscience than a cat and no more scruples than a skunk.

But in fairness to the animal kingdom, animals were generally cleaner and healthier than I was then.

I had hit the bottom branch by now and the ground was rushing up to meet me. Soon, it would be over.

When darkness falls on the Zone each night, this wretched part of the city is strangely transformed. It almost looks as if a great swarm of fireflies have settled into a country meadow, the dark interrupted by the tiny flickers of light from a thousand glowing bodies.

Of course, there are no fireflies in the zone on a summer night.

The flickers come from the lighting of a thousand crack pipes, the literal dark intruded upon by a different, more hopeless form of darkness that only masquerades as light.

I wasn't afraid of the dark any more, as I had been as a little girl. It was now what I lived for. It was all I lived for.

Chapter 9
"Mobbin and Robbin"

Late one night, as I was sitting in the park, a man named Bill found me and told me to come with him. Bill or "Pops" was one of the oldest of the street people; he'd been living on the streets in the Zone for years and years and knew everything there was to know about surviving in this environment.

Pops took me to another little seedy hotel, which was also across the street from the park on Van Buren.

"You got no business out in the streets," he said, ushering me into his room at the hotel.

Pops got me some clothes and something to eat. Then we got high together. He said I reminded him of his daughter and from that point we had sort of a father-daughter relationship.

Pops took me on a tour of the Zone the next day. We stopped by Interfaith, a charity that provides clothes to the homeless and to St. Vincent De Paul – Vinny's is what street folks called it – and The Andre House. Between Vinny's and The Andre House, you could get three meals a day, provided you got in line early. They always ran out of food before they ran out of hungry homeless people. He also took me by the Central Arizona Shelter Services (CASS) where, if you were lucky, you could sleep with a roof over your head. Of course, with a limited number of beds CASS was strictly first-come, first-serve, so it wasn't much of long-term option.

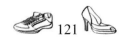

As we moved around the Zone, Pops offered me advice and tips about how to live on the streets. He told me who to avoid and who I could approach. Everyone seemed to know Pops. His years on the streets earned him respect; nobody ever tried to pick on him, even though he was an old man.

I met quite a few people through Pops and before long; I felt comfortable enough to strike out on my own.

I got to know several of the dope dealers in the neighborhood – guys like Cowboy, Gordo, Grande, Palone and Marco and I soon discovered that my old hustle in Flagstaff would work here, too.

The dealers did not trust the white people who would cruise through the Zone in search of dope. They had all seen too many cases where the white client was really an undercover cop or an immigration agent.

So whenever a white person would be spotted in the neighborhood looking for dope, I served as the liaison between customer and dealer. I would approach the customer, ask him what he wanted, take his money, go make the purchase and return with the dope.

I usually ended up with some dope or money, sometimes both. If a guy gave me $100, I would buy $60 or $70 worth of dope and pocket the rest. When I returned with the dope, the customer would either give me some of the dope or pay me.

It was a hustle that worked pretty well. I was able to stay high most of the time and sometimes I'd have enough money to rent a hotel room.

There were times when I could have escaped that life, if I had been willing. One of those opportunities came when I happened to be standing on a corner when a car pulled up. The man in the passenger side seat asked if I knew where I could get a $20 rock. I told him I could make that happen, taking his $20 bill and running to the dope house. When I returned, he asked me my name. He told me his name was Clarence, but everybody called him "C." He said he'd be back in a little while, but I didn't see him again until about a week later.

Again, he pulled up in a car. Again, I ran off to get the dope. When I returned, he said he'd be back in about 30 minutes. He seemed awfully nervous to me and I assumed, correctly it turned out, that he was a working man, the kind of guy who just smokes on the weekends and doesn't want anyone to know about it.

This arrangement went on for a while. Then one day, I was told there was a man in the park looking for me. Nobody knew the guy, which aroused their suspicions, but he told them he was looking for his sister, Brenda. From that point on, everyone thought we were siblings.

As it turned out, "C" really did become a big brother to me. As he became more addicted, he spent more and more time in the Zone. He began to watch out for me; in fact, he got into fights to protect me, even went to jail in my place once.

We got high together for a few months, until "C" figured he had enough. He told me he wanted to quit using and that he was going home. He asked me to come with him.

He called his girlfriend, Dee, and she picked us up and drove us back to their apartment. Dee was an angel to me. She gave me some clothes and fixed up a place for me in one of their bedrooms. Soon it was if we were a family. I loved the idea of not having to pack my clothes around in a shopping cart or backpack. I loved being able to take a shower whenever I wanted.

Dee did everything she could think of to help "C" and me, but in the end neither of us were really ready to turn our back on our addiction.

Soon, I was back on the street. I'd still get high with my brother "C", but he soon developed his own circle of friends.

It was often feast or famine in the dope game. The feast times presented challenges, too. When the money and crack were flowing, I'd spend days on never-ending crack binges then go to sleep in what addicts refer to as a cocaine coma for three or four days, either in the park or under the 7th Avenue Bridge.

Back then, the 7th Avenue Bridge was almost like a hostel for the homeless. It was considered to be one of the few safe places to sleep, mainly because so many homeless people congregated there and because it was one of the few well-lit areas in the Zone.

We would sleep on old mattresses or cushions we found in trash bins or, when we couldn't find that, we sleep on plastic garbage bags or cardboard. I knew a lot of the guys who slept under the bridge, so I always felt as though I could lie down and sleep and be safe.

Safety is a relative thing on the streets, though. Lord knows, there were plenty of times when my hustle put me in dangerous situations. Getting into a car with a stranger is always a gamble. I had a man pull a knife on me, had a gun pointed at me and had to fight off more than a few would-be rapists. I got into a lot of fights over drugs and drug deals gone wrong, with men and women alike.

But by then I was so deep into my addiction that I just looked at those dangers as occupational hazards. I was too far gone to see the insanity of my situation, I guess.

Of course, there was also a matter of getting arrested. I went to jail a few times for petty crimes like trespassing or attempting to possess crack cocaine. I'd spend a few days or weeks in jail. When I was released I always headed straight to the dope house on 15th Avenue and Polk to see Grande, one of my favorite dealers. If you showed Grande your release papers, he would give you free dope. It was a business strategy for him: he knew if you got some dope, you would be back for more soon enough. It was the singular driving force in my life. Sometimes, I would fall in with some guys who had a car and we would make "beer runs." Two of them would go into the convenience store. One person would go to the counter and keep the cashier occupied while the other person would go back to the beer cooler, grab as much beer as he could carry and run out of the store, without paying.

My job was to stay outside the store and keep an eye out for cops. I was the getaway driver.

In addition to the beer, I would often ask the guys to grab cigarettes, Mad Dog 20/20, and sometimes even tampons as part of my share of the booty.

Beer runs were just one of my criminal enterprises.

For about a year, Tony and I worked a hustle that suited our own unique talents.

Tony grew up in New York, one of six kids. His dad died when he was young and that loss had a profound effect on him. There was always a rage that burned deep inside him and as he grew into manhood, that rage would erupt into great spasms of violence.

He first came to Phoenix as part of a construction crew working on a building project. By then, he was in his late 30s and had been smoking weed and crack since he was a teenager. When he got to Phoenix, he took one look around and decided on the spot he was going to stay. He told me later that the weather was so nice year-round that he felt like he was on a permanent vacation. He figured he'd just stay on the streets and get high all the time. And that's exactly what he did.

Tony survived on animal instincts. Although he wasn't tall – just 5-foot-9 - he was powerfully built, with a thick muscular chest and arms. Beyond his physical strength, his attitude made him a man to be feared on the streets. He lived by a simple, brutal code: If you had something he wanted, he was going to take it. You could either give it up or he could take it from you. He didn't care either way.

People on the street were wary of Tony and when he and I began to hang out, many of my friends tried to tell me to stay away from him. Somehow, though, I saw something in him that other people couldn't see. I knew I would be safe with Tony, that he would never hurt me. And, for once, I was right.

I realized that Tony's fierceness could be used to score money and drugs. Soon, we developed a hustle we called "Mob and Rob."

We would scrape together enough money to get a room in a cheap hotel on the east side of Van Buren Street and I would go out and stand on the street corner like a prostitute to meet a trick (men) and lure him back to the room under the pretense that we would have sex for money.

Tony and I had a signal that let him know when the money had been exchanged between the trick and me. We would get into the room and discuss what he wanted and how much it was going to cost him. When I had the money I would open and close the curtain which was the signal for Tony to come busting through the door. At my signal, Tony would suddenly burst into the room in a rage, screaming about what happened to any man he caught with "his woman." Believe me, in that agitated state, Tony was a fearsome spectacle. The men would always break down the door to get out of the room, never even thinking about getting their money back.

It was a pretty good hustle. It worked every time. Only rarely did anyone ever dare stand up to Tony. And on those occasions, the outcome was always predictable. The trick would leave broke, both physically and financially.

It was a pretty good hustle for a while. Tony and I lived large, which in our world meant we got to stay in cheap hotel rooms and stay high. We were not a couple, but we had a good relationship. We were both friends and business partners.

Tony and I would part ways and hang out with other people and then connect again when we ran into each other and rob and mob. Eventually I got to the point at that stage of the crack game that I simply had quit caring. For me, the only thing that mattered was the next hit on a crack pipe and I had a drive to get high that was almost frightening. No matter how sorry my condition, I was able to get high, often going on crack binges that lasted for days.

When those binges were over, I'd stumble away and find a place to sleep. If I was lucky, I'd make it to the relative safety of the 7th Ave. Bridge. Other times, I'd find a few cushions, a discarded sofa; even a broken down refrigerator and make a crude sort of nest and sleep there. Sometimes, I'd just pass out and sleep on the grass at Jurassic Park.

And this was no ordinary sleep, either. Crack addicts call it a "cocaine coma." You simply pass out and don't wake up, sometimes for days. When someone is in a cocaine coma, it is almost impossible to wake them.

On one such occasion, I slipped into a cocaine coma at Jurassic Park. I was obviously too far gone to choose a suitable place to sleep, because I happened to lie down squarely on top of an ant bed. Thousands of ants soon began to swarm over my body. But I was already in my cocaine coma and never felt a bite. Sometime later, Tony was walking through the park and happened to notice me stretched out on the grass and came over to check on me. What he saw horrified him: Ants were swarming all over my body, leaving nasty welts on every inch.

He managed to rouse me enough to get me to my feet and carried me, still covered in ants, across the street to an empty room at the City Center hotel. He put me in the shower to wash the ants off my body. Ant bites covered me entirely. My face was swollen and discolored; I looked like I'd been beaten. There were ant bites inside my ears and nostrils, even my mouth and tongue.

I might very well have died, if Tony had not happened by.

Of course, I figured that his arrival was, at best, a dubious blessing. Dying of ant bites was as good a way to go as any, I figured, especially if I didn't wake up as it was happening. The day finally came when my partnership with Tony was broken. Tony and I had been spending days and weeks together and we finally talked about our feelings towards one another. I was definitely attracted to him just as he was to me but we never acted on our feelings. We made the decision that we loved each other and wanted to be together. We had been up for a few days so we decided to go and get a room at the Desert Inn. We were going to get high and take our relationship to the next level, however it never happened. Tony went into the bathroom and I fell asleep. So much for a romantic night together! That happened to also be our last time together as partners in crime. The next day Tony was arrested on drug charges and sent away to serve a five-year prison sentence.

Chapter 10
"Losing My Shoes"

It had been 12 years since the afternoon I came home from work to find Mel and Stanley smoking crack cocaine in a back bedroom of my Flagstaff apartment. A dozen years had passed since I took that first hit on a crack pipe and began an insane journey into the abyss.

There was no real need to do an inventory of all the things I had lost in my insatiable pursuit of the next high. Better, simpler, is to say I lost everything and leave it at that.

Even in the drug-induced haze that had become my usual condition, I realized that there would be a day that I'd take my last hit on a crack pipe. And as time went by, I was certain that day was just over the horizon.

I had long since given up on the idea that I'd simply quit using; there had been too many false hopes and failures to keep that fantasy alive.

I would quit smoking crack the day I died.

Until then, I just drifted, detached from the world. Life seemed cheap, worthless, and this seemed to be a common view among the people living in the Zone.

You saw it in the blank stares of the homeless. You saw it as you walked along the alleys, where prostitutes performed their sex acts in plain view and in broad daylight. You saw it in the crack houses and dope houses and under the 7th Avenue Bridge.

129

Nobody cared. Everybody was waiting, killing time as they killed themselves.

Everybody seemed to be waiting for That Day.

I was convinced my day had come in August of 1996.

Tony had been taken to jail that morning. Within a few hours, I was hanging out underneath the 7th Avenue Bridge considering my options. I had been there for a while when the guy we called "Van Dyke" came by, looking for me.

"You want to go down to the D.I. and get high?" he asked.

It was early afternoon when we arrived at the D.I. and we immediately started to smoke crack and drink wine. A while later, one of Van Dyke's friends came down from his room down the hall. He was an older man, probably in his 60s, I guessed. He was smoking a combination of weed and crack he had rolled into a blunt.

I wasn't really paying much attention to him, though, although I did hear Van Dyke and the man talking quietly in the corner of the room.

Van Dyke came over, sat on the bed and lit his pipe and the man stood by the doorway, apparently uncertain if he was going to stay or go.

"Hey," Van Dyke whispered to me. "My friend says he has some dope and some money and he wants to be with you. He said he'd give you anything you wanted."

I took a hit from my pipe and looked up.

"But I'm saving myself for marriage," I said.

Van Dyke just looked at me, a blank expression on his face.

I chuckled.

"I won't have sex with him," I said. "I'll get high and party with him, but as far as being with him goes, I'm not going to go there. Period. End of story."

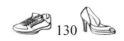

Given my state, it's hard to know why I was so firm on that issue. Lord knows, I'd pretty much abandoned every other scruple I had ever held. Somehow, though, selling my body was a line I couldn't seem to cross.

Once I had shot down the man's proposal, it seemed as though it was a dead subject. Van Dyke and the man never asked again.

So we went back to the business at hand.

After a few more hours of smoking and drinking, the man asked me if I wanted a Demerol.

I was well acquainted with Demerol from the weeks after I had been shot. Although pills weren't my drug of choice, I did like to take them when I was smoking and drinking.

So I took the Demerol the man offered and continued to smoke and drink.

Before long, I began to suspect that the pill the man had given me wasn't Demerol at all. I started to hallucinate. I began to feel dizzy. I began to feel nauseous.

"Hey!" I said, and that is all I remember. I passed out before I could even finish the sentence.

I do not know how long I was asleep. The next memory I have is suddenly being aware of something heavy pressing down on me.

I opened my eyes to see the form of a man. I could feel the heat of his breath near my face and was aware of a violent jerking motion of his body against mine as I lie on the floor of a darkened room.

The fog of whatever drug I had been given left me disoriented so that I did not immediately grasp what was happening. The man grunted and thrust his body against mine.

I was being raped.

Rational thought abandons you when you are in that situation. Your mind, at first, is an explosion of jagged emotions: Terror, panic, outrage, disgust.

Fight, scratch, push, kick, my mind commanded but my body would not respond. I tried to scream, but words would not come.

I stared up at the dark figure on top of me, but I could see only the silhouette of the man. I could not identify him; his features were hidden in the darkness.

And in a way, it was the most awful part of it all. Was this a stranger, or was it someone I knew, someone I saw every day? I hated the thought that I would never know. Because he wasn't a particular man, he could be any man I knew, any man I'd ever know. I might turn a corner one day and bump into this monster and never know it.

I would never be safe.

He would be there in the dark.

Forever.

He must have noticed that I was conscious, because for a moment he stopped the assault – but only for a moment. Satisfied, I guess, that I was powerless to resist, he continued his attack, grunting like some sort of animal, slamming his flesh against mine.

I tried to look around the room in a desperate hope that there would be someone who might intervene.

A corner of the room was illuminated by the street light that peaked through the battered slates of the Venetian blinds. By that light, I could see the form of a man sitting on the corner of a bed, smoking a cigarette. I tried to catch his gaze and I could see that he was looking in my direction.

He just sat there, smoking his cigarette.

It seemed like the last thin veneer of humanity had been stripped away and I realized what I had become. Or rather, what I wasn't. I wasn't a person anymore, but an object, something to be used and discarded. Everything I had come to believe about myself during my wretched years on the streets was suddenly confirmed. I was nothing.

The man on top of me continued to jam his body against mine, grunting and sweating and stinking and I hated what was happening. I hated him. I hated me and what I had become.

The man on the bed crushed out his cigarette in an ashtray, picked up his crack pipe and starting smoking. I saw him look at me and then look away.

That's the last thing I remember about that night.

I woke up on a couch in the alley off Garfield Street, and it all came back to me. I saw the dead cat next to the sofa and began to have dry heaves, furious, body-convulsing heaves that turned my stomach muscles into knots and scraped my throat raw. About the only thing I had had in my stomach was the cheap wine we had been drinking the night before and the stench of my vomit was close to unbearable. I closed my eyes, exhausted, and rolled back onto the sofa, hoping to pass out and never, ever wake up again.

Let me die, I silently pleaded with God. *Please.*

But as the unrelenting sun bore into my weary body, I realized that I would neither sleep nor die. You have to be pretty lucky to die, I thought.

And since I wasn't going to be lucky, my thoughts turned to easing my suffering. My first thought was that I had to get some water. I knew I was badly dehydrated and I knew that I had to get some water soon. I figured my best bet was to go to University Park, which was about a mile away. I had friends there. They would take care of me. I'd be safe.

133

I sat up and looked down at my feet.

"Hey, where are my shoes?" I thought, looking around on the ground to see if, perhaps, I had kicked them off at some point during the night. But my shoes were nowhere to be found. Either those low life rat bastards had carried me barefoot into the alley and left me here, or someone else had stolen my shoes while I as passed out. I began to cry, deep sobs with no tears, for I don't how long.

Calmer now and better able to think clearly, I told myself I had to get out of that alley. That meant I was going to have to walk barefoot to the park. I rose up from the sofa and began to walk down the dirt alley strewn with broken glass, syringes and feces. Weak and dizzy, I tried to pay careful attention to where I walked, but it was impossible to avoid stepping on the shards of glass, which were obscured by a thin layer of dust. I could feel the cuts of the glass as I walked, but there was nothing I could do but press on.

Halfway down the alley, I looked back to see the faint trail of bloody footprints. I tried to ignore the pain from my bleeding feet as I walked, focusing my attention on the end of the alley, eager to reach the sidewalk, where I'd be able to see what lay under each footstep.

But as soon as I reached the sidewalk, I found that I had traded one misery for another.

The first step onto the sidewalk felt as though I had just put my foot on the eye of a hot stove. I winced in pain with each step. Maybe I can run, I thought, but I soon found that I didn't have the strength. Step by searing step, I staggered down the sidewalk. After a half-block, I noticed a temperature gauge that was hanging on the side of one battered house and noted the temperature: 115 degrees.

My feet were already badly blistered and I had only walked a few hundred yards. I looked down the street, to see if there was any part of the sidewalk that was shaded by the few trees that grew stubbornly along the street. But the sun was directly overhead. There was no shade that I could see, so I began to look for little pockets of sand that had collected on the sidewalk. The sand, though hot, was a lot better than the smoldering pavement.

At great intervals, I'd find a little patch of sand to stand on. Usually, it was too small a patch to stand on with both feet. So I would stand on the sand on one foot and hold my other foot off the ground until I lost my balance. Then I'd switch feet. I tried this pathetic hop-scotch down the street, but soon found the little patches of sand more and more scarce.

At one point, I saw a Doritos bag that had been pinned by the wind against a chain-link fence. I slipped the bag over the foot that seemed to be most painful and walked a few steps, hoping that the thin cellophane bag would offer some small respite from the pain. But the bag kept slipping off my foot and finally tore apart.

I could see the park in the distance, less than a quarter-mile away. It seemed like a thousand miles to me.

The pain was almost constant now. I could feel blisters rising on the bottom of my torn feet. My throat was so dry I felt as though I was beginning to choke. The sun seemed to be burning my flesh away. I was dizzy and felt faint and feared that I might simply collapse there on the sidewalk.

I continued staggering down the sidewalk toward the park. I could feel the tears on my cheeks as I inched closer to the park. But even if I got to the park, what would it matter, I began to think. Life wasn't worth living anyway.

I pushed those thoughts aside and kept going.

Even all these years later, there are some things I don't understand about that day.

For one thing, the houses along my route from the alley to the park were houses I had been in. I had gotten high in just about every one of these houses and knew the people who lived there. At any time, I could have escaped my misery by simply walking into one of those houses and all of my immediate needs would have been met. It seems so obvious now.

Strange, too, that I never encountered anyone on that walk. Just about any other day, there were people out, pushing their shopping carts along the sidewalk or driving by.

But on this day, there was no one on the street, no one to help me.

Without the searing pain, I might easily have convinced myself that it was all a hideous dream. There was, indeed, something almost ethereal about it, as if I were predestined for the moment, that there was some larger purpose, some greater force that was driving me blindly on.

The park was just a few dozen agonizing steps away now and I could feel myself losing control of my emotions. I begin to cry again as I staggered onto the cool grass of the park and collapsed.

A few of my friends – Bill, Westside, and Glen - found me. Between sobs, I tried to tell them what had happened. Bill sent Glen to get water to wash and clean my feet. Westside ran two miles to his aunt's house and came back with a pair of flip-flops.

Although I was no longer on the burning sidewalk, my feet still felt as though they were burning. Bill poured water over my feet and gently washed them, careful not to put too much pressure on the burned, cut and badly swollen flesh. After he had cleaned my feet, he applied some Vaseline in hopes that it would help stem the flow of blood from the many cuts, and then slipped a pair of socks over my feet.

Westside had also brought me some clothes to wear, throwing the sweat and vomit drenched clothes I had been wearing into a trash can.

The three men lifted me and carried me to the part of the park that was shaded by some large trees. They put a blanket down for me and then sat down around me. One of them offered me a bottle of Mad Dog 20/20 wine. I drank the whole bottle in gulps, stretched out on the blanket and passed out.

I must have slept for a few hours. When I awoke Bill, Glen and Westside were sitting around me smoking crack. They didn't notice that I was awake right away because I didn't try to get up at first.

Again, there was something dream-like about the world into which I had awakened, as if I was looking at the scene from some distance, or sitting in a movie theater and watching a film.

I gazed in one direction and saw a pregnant homeless woman hitting on a crack pipe, then vomiting, and then hitting the pipe again. I looked another direction and saw another woman with several young children lying down under the shade of some old wooden bleachers. As I scanned my surroundings, I saw old men drinking beer as they pushed all of their earthly belongings through the park in battered shopping carts. I saw an old woman digging in the garbage looking for aluminum cans. I saw people getting high who looked like they might fall over from an overdose at any moment.

I sat up and carefully pulled the socks off my feet so I could examine them in horror. They were bloody and blistered. I thought to myself, *What have you done? What have you become? Why?*

Then I asked God why. And felt faint stirrings within me.

 137

My friends noticed that I was awake. One of them offered me the crack pipe. I looked at it as if I were some strange object that I had never seen before.

He held it out there as I studied the pipe, waiting for me to accept it.

"No," I said, startled by my response. It was probably the first time in 12 years that I had said "no" to an offer of crack. I was not myself, I realized. Brenda never turns down a hit on a crack pipe.

My friends seemed startled, too, but no one spoke. They continued to pass the pipe around to each other.

I got up and walked away from them, to the middle of the park where I could be alone. I had to figure out what had happened, what it meant.

I could feel a lump swelling in my throat and hot tears began to stream down my cheek as I stood there, alone, in the middle of the park. Then at once, I fell to my knees. I heard my voice crying out to God.

"I can't go on," I said. "Not another day, not another hour, not another second. I can't!"

Somehow, I knew – absolutely knew – that I would be dead if I had to live as an addict even one more day.

I thought of all the horrible things I had done, all the people I had hurt.

"Please, Jesus, forgive me," I begged. "Help me. I don't know what I'm supposed to be doing with my life, but it can't be this. All I know is I don't want to live this way, I don't want to be homeless on the streets, and I don't want to be on crack. Help me!"

My anguish reached a point that I couldn't even form words. I collapsed on my face, sobbing so hard that I could feel my body shaking. All of the sordid events of my life began to play through my head and I hated the person I had become. I didn't know what happened to the real Brenda; I could hardly remember that person anymore. But I wanted to go back, to be that girl, somehow. I wanted to be free of that life of drugs that I had been a slave to all these years. I wanted to recover and do something positive with my life, whatever that might be.

All this time, I thought I had wanted to die, but I realized that what I really had been crying out for just the opposite. I wanted to live, really live.

"God, help me," I murmured over and over.

I don't know how long I lay there on the grass, repeating myself. But after a while, I began to feel a sense of relief. Warmth began to seep into my heart, and nourish my soul.

I sat up and looked around me. I heard birds singing. Had they always been there, I wondered? I felt a breeze against my cheek. The tops of the trees seemed to dance in the wind and it seemed so magical to me. I watched the clouds move across the sky and felt a chill of appreciation run through my body. I looked around. How impossibly green did the grass look now. What wonderful colors exploded all around me.

This was University Park. I had been here a thousand times. But it was different than before. I was different, but I couldn't define how.

The suffocating pain that had haunted me every day during of my life on the streets was gone, as though a knife had been removed from my back. I felt as though shackles had fallen from my hands and feet.

A gentleness enveloped me and I felt that it was God wrapping his arms around me, holding me close, telling me that I was safe now, that I was forgiven, that I was free.

I look at my blistered, burned, cut feet. I thought about how I was still homeless. But I also knew that something profound had happened. I was different. I had been changed.

Just like that.

I was suddenly aware that I was smiling and, for the first time in a long time, the smile was not a mask.

"I am free!"

Part 3

A picture is worth a thousand words!

Lillie Slater (grandma)

Mama

Daddy

Walter

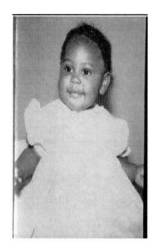 

Brenda

The Combs family

Mom and Dad

Walter & Hazel

Sharon, Dwight, Brenda First Baptist Church Children's Choir

High School Graduation   Stanley Joyce

Brenda, Jackie, & Pam   Walter & Brenda

Uncle Perry, Uncle Terry and me   Lee Phillips Attorney at Law

1985 Crack Cocaine days

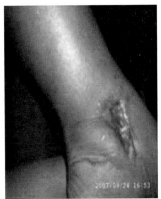

Mug shot   Gunshot wound

The look of 10 years of homelessness and addiction

Inmate "Tony" Carter

Jose and Brenda

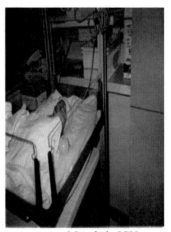

Mycole in ICU

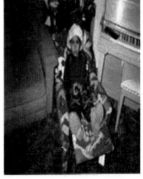

Mycole

Under the bridge

My students

Combs family

Bell family

My first home

Master of Special Education

2007 GCU Graduation   Sistah's Beth, Brenda & Terri

MLK Stand Up For Justice Award   Headed to the Inauguration

Community Event w/ Shaq   Power To End Stroke Awards 2009

 154

National Hunger/Homeless Awareness Day Finding My Shoes Event

AZ Women of Inspiration/Jackie Joyner-Kersee   "Pops"

Brenda & Tony

brother Clarence, Bonita & Tony

Reader's Digest 2007

Christmas 2008

Carter family 2009

Chapter 11
"Potholes on the Yellow Brick Road"

As I stood there in the park that afternoon, the glorious feeling of newfound strength gave way to gentle gratitude. God hadn't given up on me. I said a silent prayer. *Thank you for seeing something good and special within me.*

Then I began to plan out my next steps. Whatever I decided to do, I had better do quickly. Even one more day on the streets was a dangerous prospect. I feared that this change I experienced might fade away, especially if I stayed in the same environment, a place where it is ridiculously easy to find drugs.

I considered the few options that seemed available and, for once, chose the least pleasant one: I decided to turn myself into the probation department. I knew what the consequences would be. Most likely there was a warrant out for my arrest, and my probation officer would be duty bound to report me to the police.

I chose not to focus on the thought of going back to jail - enduring the degradation of the Horseshoe and, after that, the mind-numbing monotony of incarceration. Once I was released from jail, I could get into a rehab program. Previously, the thought of going through rehab was almost as unpleasant as going to jail. Now, I saw it in a different, more hopeful light. I suppose that was the first manifestation that the change I had experienced there at the park was not only real, but enduring.

I hobbled on my badly injured feet, wincing from pain, and headed down Roosevelt Avenue toward Andre House. That's

where I hoped to get a meal before going to the probation office. I had not eaten in more than 24 hours and in my weakened condition, it was likely I would faint if I didn't eat soon.

I didn't bother telling anyone about what had happened to me or about my plans to turn myself in. I knew no one would believe me, and I understood why they wouldn't.

But it didn't really seem to matter anymore.

As I was walking, someone ran up and said that Jose was in the neighborhood looking for me. I wasn't really anxious to see him, though; I had walked out on him without explanation and was afraid there would be a confrontation. I didn't need the drama. I made it to Andre House and got some food, then made my way to the probation office. As I was walking, I saw Jose pedaling towards me on a bicycle.

When he reached me, he jumped off the bike and hugged me. I was sort of paralyzed for a moment, not sure what his intentions might be. He asked me what I was doing, but I couldn't respond. He must have noticed that there was something unusual, even mysterious, in my demeanor.

It didn't seem to matter to Jose. He told me that he loved me and wanted to help me. He said he didn't care what I had done, what had happened before. He loved me and wanted to support me, provided I was willing to give up the streets.

I told Jose where I was going, to the probation department, to turn myself in. He walked with me there. When I arrived, I related to my probation officer everything that had happened in the past 24 hours – about the rape, losing my shoes, the long tortured walk to the park. I told her I was ready to get off the streets, even if it meant going to jail.

Michelle listened patiently. For a couple of minutes she said nothing. Then she looked into my eyes. "You did a brave thing coming in here. You're finally making that change, Brenda, yes, you are. " She gave me a big grin.

"I know I probably have a warrant," I said.

She didn't respond. All she said was, "Come back and see me on Monday." It was late Friday afternoon.

"Come back Monday?" I asked, perplexed. I was certain that I was going to be arrested on the spot. I had counted on it.

For the first time in my life, I was worried about the prospects of *not* spending a weekend in jail. Where would I go? I knew going back into the Zone was not an option. The very idea terrified me.

Jose couldn't help me. He was AWOL from the rehab facility he was living at and had to get back before he was discovered missing.

I left the probation office and stood on the sidewalk, trying to figure out what I could do. My family would help me. I decided to call Dwight. He worked downtown, not far from where I was standing. He told me to come over to his office.

I walked the short distance to Dwight's workplace. By the time I arrived, he had already talked to our sister Sharon , and they had a plan. He drove me to Sharon 's apartment where, for the first time in what seemed like ages, I was able to lie down and sleep in a safe environment. I must have been in a cocaine coma, because I slept the entire weekend.

When I woke up, it was Monday, time to go back to the probation office and, shortly after that, jail.

Michelle, my probation officer sat down with me and we talked for a while. She spoke to me with kindness and respect. Her focus seemed to be entirely on what options I had and what my future plans might be. There was no talk of jail at all.

Finally, I cut to the chase. "Am I going to be arrested?"

She leaned back in her chair. "My supervisor wanted me to issue a warrant on you when you came here on Friday, but I put it off," she said. "Truth is, going to jail isn't going to do you any good. All you have done really is violate probation and going to jail hasn't ever been much of a deterrent for you."

She paused again. "You are going to have to take control of your life," she said. "I believe you can do it, Brenda. But it's really all up to you."

She didn't have to tell me twice. I was out the door a few minutes later and on my way to the Center for Healing in Glendale. The Center for Healing was a co-ed residential facility, run by the residents with the supervision of a live-in house manager.

Although it was a new program, I was skeptical. Like most of the other rehab facilities I had lived in, Center for Healing was filled with people who don't really want to be there – folks who have been sent to the program on court orders. Very few residents were there by choice.

That makes a huge difference. You can force people to go to rehab, but you simply cannot force them to quit using. In every program I had ever been in, people were using drugs. For most, it was a cycle: Get in the program, get clean, and then relapse. And it seemed just about if anyone had a relapse, it would spread through the house like an epidemic.

So it was hard to stay clean, even in rehab.

Of course, this was no surprise to the staff. Molly, who was like the house mother, would show up unannounced and do random drug tests. Without fail, there would be some residents who failed the test and were asked to leave. Almost every roommate I had during my 90-day stay at Center for Healing was asked to leave because of a failed drug test. When I arrived, I shared a room with three women. By the time I left, I had the room to myself.

Life at Center for Healing was pretty much what you find at most programs of its kind. You were required to either work or spend your day looking for work. You had to pay rent - $90 per week. You were required to perform household chores. And, finally, you were required to attend daily programs, which included A.A. and N.A. meetings.

Residents were on their own for food, although you did have access to the kitchen.

While I was at the Center, I went to work at different call centers and collection agencies. These were not exciting positions, but the offices were close by and they didn't do background checks. Because I was making only slightly more than the minimum wage, I had to be very frugal. I got most of my food from Interfaith or St. Mary's Food Bank, and I shopped for clothes at Goodwill.

I talked to my brother and sister on the phone every now and then and also wrote letters to my parents. My parents drove to Phoenix regularly to visit. Whereas before, all they could do was put me on their prayer list at church, and ask "that God would put the drug dealers out of business, help the police to shut down the dope houses, and take the taste for drugs out of Brenda's mouth." They were happy that I was alive and in treatment. My mother would tell me every time I saw her how grateful she was that I had turned myself in. She believed that God had spared my life.

They were extremely supportive, but it was also obvious that they were cautious, too. I realized, of course, that anything I said to my family was likely to be taken with a healthy measure of skepticism. They had heard it all before. They would pitch in and help me out whenever I asked, but I was not quick to do so, because I felt I had no right after all I had put them through. I also really wanted to be independent and take care of things myself.

Through it all, I felt pretty much alone. I realized that it is pretty hard for people who have never been addicts to really understand what it's like to come out of that kind of darkness. I was starting over. For a lot of people this is just too much. It's one thing to start at the bottom. Most people who are coming off drugs understand that it's going to be that way. What I believe is the greater danger is the very real prospect that you might never come out at all.

I looked at my life. Even living in a facility, I was barely scratching by. If there was a brighter future out there, it seemed almost impossible to imagine how to get there from where I was.

It is not only hard, which addicts expect, but sometimes it seems almost hopeless. And it is at that point where a lot of people, me included, simply give up.

In my previous trips to rehab, I had always lived with the fear that I would be one of the many who simply crack under that kind of pressure.

But this time was different. As hard and hopeless as this new life was at times, I held on to the unshakeable conviction that I was a changed person.

But I found that even that conviction presented a challenge.

Really, it all came down to tense. In addition to the mandated meetings, I was also attending out-patient counseling. To me I was "recovered." But the counselors and even the other residents were equally convinced that I was "recovering." Big difference. More than one counselor said I'd be back on the streets in six months if I could not admit that I was a "recovering addict."

The path of least resistance would have been to simply agree with them and chalk it off as a matter of semantics. But deep

down, I could not force myself to say that I was a "recovering addict." I was convinced that God had healed me. Somehow, saying I was "recovering" seemed a denial of that. I simply could not, would not, go there.

For quite a while, I tried to articulate what had happened to me that day in alley and in the park. Oh, they could sympathize and understand the physical trauma of my tortured walk from that alley to the park. They could understand the horror of walking that distance on bloodied, blistered feet. They could understand the pain of being drugged and raped and left for dead in an alley.

But those were the external realities of the story. What they could not see, what I could not convey to them, was that something even more dramatic had taken place inside me. A miracle had taken place inside me. And in an instant, I had become a new person. I had passed from death to life in a profoundly spiritual way.

But the truth is, I was working my program. And I was as committed to the "12 Steps" of Alcoholics Anonymous as any resident. Although I grew to absolutely despise the meetings. Listening to resident after resident stand up and talk about the eight-ball they had smoked the weekend before was, to me, a colossal waste of time. I wanted strategies, solutions. The meetings never got within a mile of that. Or at least the meetings I attended at that time. This was years before I discovered Celebrate Recovery which is a spiritual aspect of a 12 step meeting.

What I would not realize until later is that not all A.A. meetings are the same. It's like anything else, the ingredients determine the outcome. I learned that living in a halfway house with a bunch of drug addicts and alcoholics can be just as challenging as living on the streets with a bunch of addicts and alcoholics. The value of the meetings depends on the sincerity of those who attend. Suffice to say, in this particular instance, sincerity was in short supply. And the irony of it is that one of the most sincere people in the program was considered to be the least committed.

There were times that I felt like simply running away. But there was no place to run to. I also realized that I could not be a prisoner to the opinions and expectations of others. When I became discouraged and felt like it was just too hard, I told myself that God had changed me. That was the hard part. I could do this.

After three months at the Center for Healing, I lived for a couple of months in another facility – Crossroads for Women – a place that was a much better fit for me. And after that, I moved into a little apartment, eager to take the next step, encouraged and energized.

Things were looking up.

And then Jose came along.

Chapter 12
"No Way, Jose"

It is a terrible thing to be an addict. It is also a terrible thing to be married to an addict.

Not long before I left Oxford House to strike out on my own, I began to re-connect with Jose. I had known him for almost three years by then and we had been involved in an on-again, off-again relationship that started in rehab, resumed after my relapse and now emerged just as I was taking a major step in building a new life.

In Jose, I saw something of a kindred spirit. Both of us had suffered through long addictions. Both of us had managed to get sober for a while. Both of us had relapsed. From our first meeting, we had shared the deep, painful intimate secrets that are always just under the surface for any addict. And as he listened to the sordid details of my life, Jose never once condemned me or judged me. In the years that intervened, even when I learned that Jose had relapsed, I never forgot his kindness toward me.

When counselors said they had their doubts about Jose's commitment to sobriety, I thought of my own life and how many people had reached the same conclusion about me. By the time I left Oxford House, I was sure of one thing and one thing only: I was no longer an addict. And if I could beat my addiction, I knew that anyone could.

Counselors might have seen Jose as a lost cause. I could not. He was a very loving, sensitive man, always eager to please me.

He was a gentleman in all his dealings with me, someone who always seemed to put my happiness above his own. To be honest, it did not hurt his cause that he was strikingly handsome, with big brown eyes, a beautiful smile and smooth unblemished skin the color of copper.

When I was kicked out of Maverick House, Jose and I began to date and our relationship could be described as almost Victorian. We dated for a year before he proposed and waited another year to get married. During that courtship, Jose was just about everything a woman could ask for. He was doing great, staying sober and working double-shifts as a waiter. He took me out to dinner and movies and shopping. If I needed something, he was always there, eager to fill the need.

In many ways, he treated me the way Lee had treated me. I had blown it with Lee; I was determined that I wouldn't squander this opportunity with Jose.

I was determined to hold up my end of the bargain. Would Jose? As time passed, I became more and more convinced that he would.

During this time I was singing in the choir at First Baptist Church, and would sometimes go out to dinner and karaoke on Sundays with two younger friends of mine, Paul and Marcus. They didn't like Jose, and let me know it. I thought they were sweet, but they were too young to understand, and they weren't me, anyway.

A few months before our wedding, I completed my probation. With that step forward, I found myself wondering how my old friend Pops was doing. I went to my previous haunts, to the place under the bridge. He was still there. I asked him what they needed. He was hungry. I went and bought food, and brought it to him.

I found myself returning again and again. Since I was working, but not making a lot of money, I did most of my shopping at thrift stores. I often bought items in bulk, and kept them on hand at my apartment. I stocked up on soap, toothbrushes, and razors and made hygiene kits. When I found lunch meat, bread, carrots, and such, I packed sandwiches-to-go in plastic baggies. My friends from church went with me once a month, and we would deliver these items, sometimes walking around the streets and sometimes passing them out from the trunk of my car.

I would give out handwritten cards with useful Bible verses and my telephone number for people to call in case they needed something I could provide. The reason for my visits were not to cure their homelessness; the reason for my visits was to love these people where they are at. I wanted to show them that they are not throwaways to society. That they too had what it takes to make the choices and the decisions to build something with their lives. I felt like I was a living example of this. If I could do it, they could, too. Whenever I left my homeless friends in the Zone to go back to my new place, I would never say "Goodbye, see you later." I would say, "Much love." This became the basis of Much Love Ministries later on.

During all this activity, Jose was still on intense probation, meaning that his mobility was restricted, he had to attend 12 Step meetings, and he still lived at a halfway house. He wasn't allowed to go into the Zone because there were so many drugs there, and my spending time in places that he could not became a point of contention between us.

I did not recognize this until one night I was driving him back to his halfway house. We had a minor disagreement which moved into an argument and emerged as a full-blown shouting match. As I drove up to his house, Jose had become so agitated that he hit me.

I was stunned. I told him the wedding was off and peeled away from the curb.

By the time I got home, Jose was calling, apologizing and begging me to forgive him. In some ways, he seemed more shaken up by the incident than I was.

It should have been a huge red flag. Paul and Marcus pleaded with me not to take Jose back. But somehow, I couldn't walk away. Yes, I would forgive him, I decided. Jose swore to me that he had never hit a woman before and was ashamed and embarrassed of his behavior. I believed him.

I thought again of Lee, of how patient he had been, how forgiving. Now the shoe was on the other foot. Suddenly, I understood what Lee must have been feeling.

I did love Jose and I was willing to give him a second chance. My whole life was about second chances, after all.

That was, of course, a mistake. If a man hits you once, he will hit you again. You can count on it. I couldn't see it that back then, though. All I knew was that I loved Jose and desperately wanted things to work out.

We flew to Las Vegas and were married. Jose left the halfway house and we moved into a little apartment to begin our "happily ever after." In our case, Happily Ever After lasted a total of 45 days. On New Year's Eve, Jose went out, got drunk and didn't come home until 5 a.m. Happy New Year, indeed.

It was the beginning of the end. That's not to say that there were no good times; times when Jose would stay sober and be the kind loving man I knew that he could be. But before too long, those periods of sobriety became more and more the exception than the rule.

For a long time, I wanted to be that person that Jose could rely on during his struggle to stay sober. I certainly knew the difficulties of addiction, after all. In some respects, I think the circumstances were more difficult for Jose. I had been a crack addict; Jose was an alcoholic. Crack, you have to hunt for. Alcohol is everywhere you turn.

In my role as supportive wife, I went to A.A. meetings with Jose and encouraged him to work his program with his sponsor. In the meantime, I was also focusing on getting our finances and credit back in order. Jose worked as a waiter and bartender at the Biltmore and the Arizona Center and had begun to earn a reputation as a good worker.

But putting an alcoholic in an environment where he is surrounded by alcohol is never a good idea. Before long, Jose seemed more interested in drinking and getting into fights than building a new, healthy life.

That was another area where Jose and I were very different. When I was an addict, I was a happy person. I loved to sing and laugh and enjoy the people around me. Jose, on the other hand, turned out to be a "mean drunk." It was very much a Jekyll and Hyde deal for Jose. Sober, he was a sweet considerate man. Drunk, he was an explosion of violence looking for a place to erupt. All too often, that place was in our apartment.

Over our time together, the police were regular visitors to our apartment.

With more and more of Jose's money going to support his alcoholism, I realized we were going to have to find a cheaper place to live. That was a blow, because to me it represented a step back.

I found a small one bedroom apartment and gave Jose a choice: He could move in with me or stay in our old apartment. I was determined to move on with my life, with or without Jose.

On the day I moved out, Jose decided he was going to come with me.

I vowed things were going to be different. The day after we moved, Jose and I sat down and went over all of our bills. When we finished, we realized we had just enough in our checking account to cover our bills. We planned to use the tip money Jose got at his work to cover any expenses we might have until I was paid the following Friday.

That night, Jose came home so drunk that he couldn't put the key in the door. He came in and we got into a huge argument. I picked up the phone to call his sponsor, but Jose grabbed the phone, ripped it out of the wall and then moved toward me, ripping the dress I was wearing in half. I ran for the door and managed to get to the car. Jose started throwing rocks at the car as I drove off, breaking the windshield and windows. I drove to a pay phone a few hundred yards down the street and called the police.

When the police arrived, Jose was still in a rage, screaming that he was going to kill me. When the police put him in the cruiser, he tried to kick out the back windows. He was booked into jail for domestic violence.

A couple of days later, the apartment manager was at my door, telling me the check I had written for the rent had bounced. I got a sick feeling in my stomach. Jose and I had sat down just a few days before and made sure we had money in the bank to cover our expenses.

When the apartment manager left, I called the bank and was told that our checking account was overdrawn by $1,500. To make it even worse, the NSF fees hadn't been added. When it was all said and done, the total was $2,000.

Jose had emptied our account the same day we had worked out our budget.

Overnight, I had gone from being part of a two-income household to being $2,000 in debt, which seemed like a fortune at the time.

I was stunned and afraid, the images of being homeless began to come rushing back.

I went with Paul and Mel to Denny's and told them what had happened. On a whim, I asked the server if they were hiring. She said they did need some help so I applied on the spot. They put me to work right away.

I was working at a collection agency during the day. Now I had a night job waiting tables at Denny's.

I was so terrified of going back on the streets that I was willing to do anything to pay off my debts and get back on track. Often, I'd work double-shifts at the restaurant, starting at 5p.m and finishing at 5 a.m. and going home until 7:00 when it was time to report to work at the collection agency.

I continued to work the two jobs and slowly began to get back on my feet financially. In the process, I began to realize that I could, in fact, make it on my own. I didn't need someone to support me, I realized, which was a very liberating idea.

A year later when Jose got out of prison, he came back to the apartment. I knew, deep down, it was a mistake. But despite all that had happened, I still held out hope for Jose. I still believed that he could beat his addiction and that we could have a happy life together.

At first, Jose seemed committed to getting his life back on track. But before long, he began to slip. I began to realize about Jose what Lee must have finally realized about me: You can't love somebody out of an addiction.

I had reached that point. On the day I went to get the necessary paperwork to begin divorce proceedings, I came home feeling sick. I thought at first, that it was just physical response to the emotional stress I was feeling. When it didn't go away, I thought maybe I was getting the flu. My straight arrow friend, Dee, who I had met while I was hanging around with Clarence and was still friendly with, came over and listened to me as I described my symptoms.

"I bet you're pregnant," she said.

"Impossible," I answered. I had had chicken pox twice when I was in my 20s. The doctor had told me that one of the long-term effects of chicken pox among adults is that it often leaves them sterile. As a result, I had never used any birth control. I had also never gotten pregnant.

Dee listened to my explanation. "Well, it can't hurt to check, can it?" she said.

We went to the drug store, bought a pregnancy test and returned to my apartment. I almost fainted when the test showed positive. I simply couldn't believe it. On the day I had picked up the paperwork for a divorce, I had also found out I was going to have a baby.

When I told Jose, he responded by getting drunk and crying. I responded by throwing up. Dee responded by sitting in the corner, laughing hysterically.

After a doctor's visit confirmed my pregnancy, I began to worry about my baby. I was over 35 years old, with a history of thyroid disease and a 12-year addiction to cocaine. I had never considered even the possibility of being a mother, given my medical and drug history. Plus, I had a history of thyroid disease and fibrous tumors on my uterus.

I had hoped that the baby would make a change on Jose, but it seemed to affect him hardly at all. There were still many nights when he would go out and drink all night and stumble home drunk in the morning. One off the worst episodes of this was when he came home drunk and threw a magazine rack across

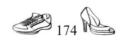

the room. It hit me in the stomach. I called 911, and Jose attacked me. My neighbor heard all the fighting and rushed in, knocked him down, and managed to restrain him until the police showed up and carted him off to jail.

Jose had violated his parole this time. He went back to prison. At that point, I would not have been able to keep food on the table and a roof over my head if my friends at church and my family had not stepped in. I drew $108 a month from welfare and was able to qualify for food stamps. Somehow, I managed, but the dreams of a bright future seemed beyond all reason.

I continued to go to the Zone and give out supplies. By now several friends had become supporters, and local businesses were willing to donate larger quantities than ever before. We turned our visits – which started off with my going to see Pops – into monthly rallies, with a choir, prayer services, hot food, and hygiene kits. Our Much Love rallies caught the attention of the news media. June Thompson of Channel Five brought a crew to film us out under the Seventh Avenue Bridge, when I was seven months pregnant with Mycole.

To compound matters, I began to have health issues of my own. I was put on bed rest at four months. Because of the heightened risks, I went to the OBGYN every week so they could monitor the baby's condition. While nothing ever showed up that was cause for concern, I realized that giving birth to a healthy child was still anything but a certainty. I tried as best I could to push my fears to the background as the time for delivery approached.

I also hoped that maybe when the baby arrived, Jose would take one look at that tiny infant and find the resolve to really make a meaningful change in his life – for Jose, for me, but mainly for the baby. I did not want my child to be raised without a father. I wanted the baby to have a home with two loving parents. I thought of my own parents, of how they had loved and supported each other through all of life's ups and downs, of how they had worked together to raise a family.

That is what I wanted for my child. Was that too much to hope for? So, despite all the evidence to the contrary, an ember of hope still flickered.

Often during my pregnancy, there were days when even getting out of bed and getting dressed seemed too great a challenge. But on the morning of January 30th, 2000, I woke up feeling surprisingly fit. I figured I would make the most of this unexpected reservoir of energy, so I began to give the apartment a thorough cleaning.

I went through the entire house – cleaning out the refrigerator, sweeping and mopping the floors, vacuuming the carpets, dusting the furniture, doing all the laundry.

When I had finished, I called Dwight and Sharon and asked if they wanted to get something to eat. They picked me up and, after a quick trip to Target to pick up a few things, we went to a restaurant. As we were eating, I felt a cramp in my stomach. I didn't think much of it; I thought maybe it was the result of all the housework. Maybe I had overdone it a bit, I figured. But another cramp followed about 30 minutes later.

Before long, the contractions came at regular intervals. I called my doctor, and then called Jose, who was at work. By now, the contractions were coming every 10 minutes. By midnight, I couldn't tell when one contraction ended and another began.

When I arrived at St. Joseph's Hospital, I was immediately taken to the birthing center. While I put on my hospital gown, Jose called everyone to tell them I was in labor.

By now, the pain was pretty intense and I was asking for my epidural. But as soon as it was administered, I began to break out in hives. It was an allergic reaction, I was told, and the staff gave me several medications to get the hives under control. Nothing seemed to work, though. At one point, they decided it would be wise to try to stop the contractions until they could get the hives under control. They also gave me pain medication and medicine to help me sleep. Twenty-four hours later, they gave me another epidural. Again, the hives returned.

Jose was long gone by that point. Under the pretense that he was going to go home and take a shower, Jose left the hospital shortly after they had decided to stop my contractions. Hours later, he called to check on me. He said he had stopped to get something to eat on the way back to the hospital. I could hear laughter and music in the background.

"I can't believe you are in a bar while I'm here about to have our baby," I said, disgusted.

While Jose was denying that he was in a bar, I heard the voice of the bartender asking Jose if he wanted another round.

I hung up the phone.

After a while, my other friends and family members began to take shifts. Finally, I was alone. I had been in labor for well over 24 hours by now and the pain of the contractions and the discomfort of the hives caused by the epidural had strained my patience to a breaking point. I begged the doctors to do a C-Section. The doctor said that he was confident that a C-Section wasn't necessary.

That didn't prevent me from asking for the C-Section each time the doctor came in to check on me, though. It went on like that for some time – me asking for a C-Section, the doctor saying it wasn't necessary. Then, suddenly, a nurse came running into my room, pulling plugs out of the wall and kicking the locks off the wheels of my hospital bed.

Puzzled by the commotion, I looked at her.

"The baby is in fetal distress," she said in a tone that at once told me something had gone terribly wrong. "We're taking you for an emergency C-Section," she said. By this point I had been in labor for 36 hours.

What followed, I can only recall in bits and pieces. I remember needles going into my arms and the anesthesiologist slipping the mask over my face. I could feel a dull sensation on my stomach, where the doctor was making the incision. Then everything went blank.

I awoke some time later, still groggy from the anesthesia. I felt my stomach and ran a finger across the incision. The fog began to lift and I called out for the nurse.

"Where's my baby?" I asked, suddenly alert.

"He's sleeping right beside you," she said.

I looked over to see my son – Mycole – sleeping in his own small bed. The nurse picked him up and placed him on my chest.

I held the tiny figure in my arms and studied him carefully. His skin was so white and he had a head full of dark hair. He was a wrinkly little guy but oh so cute. I kissed him on his head, and my heart seemed almost to ache with the love I was feeling, a love that only a mother can understand.

The rest of the day was filled with all the sights and sounds you normally associate with motherhood. Friends and family came in to see the baby. Later that day, the nurses took me down to the nursery so that I could watch Mycole get his first bath.

I remembered the alarming circumstances around his birth. Fetal distress, the nurse had said before they took me for the C-Section. That seemed terribly dangerous, but as the hours passed, there was no indication that there was anything wrong. I just figured that whatever the emergency was, it had ended when Mycole was born.

Later, I would remember something Dwight said as he was holding him.

"Hey, he's kicking me," he said, a little surprised.

I thought nothing of it, though.

Later, as the nurse was trying to help me figure out the technique of breast-feeding; I noticed that Mycole seemed to be shaking. The nurse didn't seem concerned, but later I told Jose about it. "Something's wrong," I said.

The shaking continued over the next several hours. Whenever I mentioned the shaking to a nurse, she always dismissed it as the needless worry of a new mom. "Everything's fine," they told me. "Don't worry."

But I worried anyway.

The next morning, Dr. Garcia, my family doctor, came in to visit. While he was there, Mycole began to shake again.

"He's having a seizure," Dr. Garcia said, immediately reaching for the phone and calling the nurse's station.

In a moment, the nurses were pouring into my room, grabbing Mycole out of my arms and taking him away.

When my OB/GYN came in later, I was furious. I had asked him repeatedly to perform a C-Section, but it wasn't until Mycole had gone into fetal distress that the C-Section was performed. Although I'll never know, I've always wondered if delaying the C-Section led to the seizures.

The doctors performed what seemed to be an endless series of tests on Mycole and it was heart-breaking for me when I visited the neo-natal ICU to see my child with wires and tubes all over him.

Finally, a neurologist came to my room. Jose had left and I was alone.

He sat down in a chair next to me and I could tell by his expression that we weren't about to have a casual conversation.

 179

He asked if I wanted to call someone to come and be with him as we talked. I declined. Whatever news he had, I wanted it immediately.

Mycole had had a stroke in the left frontal cortex of his brain, the neurologist told me. He said that the stroke affected the right side of Mycole's body and that the stroke was why Mycole was having seizures.

The doctor spent the next several minutes explaining Mycole's condition, but I was too overwhelmed to process much of what he said. I do remember him telling me that no one could say with any degree of certainty what the future might hold. He gave me a worst-case and best-case scenario: At worst, the stroke caused severe brain damage, seriously jeopardizing Mycole's ability to have a normal, healthy life. And even if the damage wasn't severe, there was nothing to guarantee that he would not have another stroke, perhaps even more severe, perhaps deadly.

At best, the damage might be limited to the point where the other parts of Mycole's brain could compensate for the damage. If that were true, Mycole could be expected to live pretty much a normal life, although his development might be slower than that of a normal child.

After the doctor left, I spent several minutes trying to take it all in. But it was still a jumble to me. I called the nurse and asked her to take me to see my baby.

As the nurse pushed my wheelchair from my room to the neo-natal ICU, I found myself talking to God. I didn't ask why Mycole had had a stroke. I simply asked what God what he wanted me to do now. I told God that I didn't believe what I had just been told. I knew that Mycole had a stroke, all right, but it was a lot to take in hearing that my baby had severe brain damage.

"Heal him," I prayed. "And give me whatever I need to take care of him."

I found myself looking down at my son, wires and tubes engulfing his tiny body. What kind of life would he have?   A few years earlier, I collapsed on the ground at University Park and asked for a miracle.

Now, I was asking again.

My Mycole.

My Miracle. Please, God.

Jose wasn't contributing much financially during the time Mycole was in the hospital. He would spend the money he did earn buying people drinks at the bar, but he refused to give me money to help buy food and pay rent. However, he and I did spend as much time as possible with our son, and my parents came down several times to help us out.

One afternoon my mother, Jose, and I were at the supermarket. She was helping me with my grocery shopping. Jose was preoccupied with the idea that whenever he asked about Mycole's care, the hospital staff didn't treat him with enough respect. He felt that it was because he was always dressed in a server's outfit. So he left my mother and me standing in the store aisles so he could go elsewhere and buy himself a tie. I knew that Jose had been using drugs, which is why he rushed off so strangely. My mother didn't know that.

My mother and I struggled to get the groceries to the car. When Jose arrived home later that night, we argued. My mother was upset, also, and told him, "You're not a man, just breath in a pair of pants." Their relationship never improved after that.

The change I had hoped for in my husband never came. Out of necessity, I went back to work as soon as I could. Jose worked a day shift, and I worked at Denny's at night so that we wouldn't have to pay for daycare. One night while at work, I called home to check on Mycole. Jose insisted that everything was fine, that he had just changed Mycole's diaper and given him his bottle.

I hung up, but somehow things just didn't seem right. It was nothing I could put my finger on. Call it a mother's instincts. About an hour later I decided to call again, just to be sure. No answer. I called three times. The phone just rang. I was almost in a state of panic by now. My boss allowed me to leave work early so that I could go home to check on Mycole.

I was home in a flash. As I parked, I could see that the front door of our apartment was standing open. As I walked up to the apartment, I could hear the TV blaring and I saw Mycole laying on the edge of the sofa. I called out to Jose, but no one answered. I picked up Mycole and found his diaper so soaked that it practically hanging off of him.

I looked around the apartment. No Jose. I stepped outside. Some of my neighbors were sitting outside and I asked them if they had seen Jose. They said he had left about an hour earlier.

By now, I was fuming. I went back into the apartment to call the police to report that Jose had left his infant child alone in the apartment. I changed Mycole's diaper and dressed him. I was about to lay him in his crib when I happened to run my hand over the crib sheet. I felt something like a bunch of little rocks. I turned on the light in the room and felt again, picking up the little rocks.

It was crack cocaine. A shiver went through my body. If Mycole had swallowed it, I thought…. But it was too horrible to even think about.

I called 9-1-1 and told them about the crack I had found in Mycole's crib. I gave Mycole a bottle as I waited for the police.

Jose arrived first.

He insisted that he had only been out of the apartment for a few minutes and that he had no idea of how that crack got into

the crib. It dawned on me, with a crushing finality, that we would never be a family. Our child was simply not safe with him. I bit my tongue, hoping to avoid a fight until the police arrived.

Jose went into the living room while I stayed with Mycole in the bedroom. But when I came through the living room on the way to the kitchen to get Mycole a bottle, Jose started in on me.

I had had enough. Get out, I told him.

"Make me," he said.

"I don't have to make you leave," I said. "The police will be here in a minute. I'll let them do it."

Jose went into rage; and I bolted back into the bedroom. Through the door, I could hear the crash of dishes breaking and furniture being smashed. Jose seemed to be destroying everything he could get his hands on. He threw the microwave across the kitchen, pulled out all the dishes and threw them against the wall, even smashed Mycole's high chair and ripped pictures off the walls. He went room by room, wrecking everything in sight. I could hear him ripping the shower curtain off the bar in bathroom.

He went into the second bedroom, the room I used as an office for my homeless ministry, and destroyed everything he could find. Soon, he would be in our bedroom, I realized.

I grabbed the phone to call 9-1-1 for the third time, but I could hear Jose approaching our bedroom. I raced for the door. Mycole and I had to get out of the apartment and get out now, I realized.

Clutching Mycole in my arms, I almost reached the door when Jose caught me, grabbing me by the hair, trying to drag me back into the apartment. He started hitting me with his fist. With Mycole in my arms, I was defenseless. I was screaming at him to let me go, but my pleas only seemed to enrage him all the more.

All the while, I was sure the cops would burst through the door and save us. But I suddenly realized I had to take matters into my own hands. Jose tried to slap me in the face but instead he hit Mycole and scratched his back. Mycole was only 3 months old. My baby was screaming and crying and I could see little trickles of blood coming through his shirt from being scratched. Something inside me snapped and suddenly a feeling of rage was coursing through my body. With Mycole on one hip, I began to scratch Jose and hit him with my free hand.

It was a primitive type of anger that boiled out of me. I knocked Jose to the ground and ran out the door.

I managed to get to a neighbor's apartment. A moment later, we could hear the police cruisers pulling up. Jose must have heard them too, because he managed to get to the car and drive away in the car my dad had helped me buy, just as the police were arriving. I told the police that Jose had just left and gave them the license plate number and description of the car. A whole flood of police cars were en route and one them saw Jose drive past him just as he was pulling onto the street. The officer turned around and made the stop, tackling Jose and throwing him into the back on the squad car.

At my apartment, paramedics were examining Mycole for injuries, which were confined mostly to bruises and a scratched back. They took photos of the bruises.

As the police were taking my statement, I began going through the ruins of my apartment. I noticed that the tip money was missing from my apron and that the money we had kept in drawer for the rent was missing, too.

The police had brought Jose back to the apartment while they were taking my statement. When an officer went through Jose's pockets, he found $345. Jose insisted the money was his. I told the police that the money was from my tips and our rent money.

The officer said it was my word against Jose's, and that the money would be held at the station, along with Jose's personal effects.

I begged Jose to tell them to truth. He ignored me. I asked him to leave enough money for diapers and formula, he refused. "I ain't going to jail broke," he snarled.

The next day, I went to the police station to sign an order of protection against Jose. I filed for full custody and divorce the same day.

Jose pleaded no contest to seven charges of child abuse, aggravated assault on a minor, contributing to the delinquency of a minor, child abandonment, criminal damage, assault, and a drug charge. For that, he got a sum total of one year and a half in prison. It seemed like a slap on the wrist, but there was nothing I could do.

What I could do was press on.

I had just bounced through a pretty big pothole.

Chapter 13
"Back to School"

In my mind, Mycole Rodriguez will forever be the most wonderful, amazing, incredible, beautiful human being I will ever know.

At this writing, my son is 14 years old. In most respects, he would qualify as a regular kid. He tends to be on the quiet side, although he would not be considered aloof. He's friendly, if a bit shy. Adults who know him would likely mention that he is a polite child. Teachers would tell you he is a regular kid for the most part. In all other respects, he is much like any other 14 year old boy.

But there is another quality Mycole possesses that no one could be expected to know. His calm, polite manner belies an uncommon fierceness, a tenacity that lies hidden below the happy-go-lucky exterior.

Mycole is certainly not a violent kid, but he is very much a fighter. He was a fighter from the very start. He had to be. He fought to overcome his stroke. He fought to learn how to swallow. He fought to live.

In the months before my divorce from Jose became final, for all intents and purposes I was already a single mom. In some respects, it was even worse. Jose had proven himself to be completely unreliable when it came to taking care of his family responsibilities. In fact, his presence made the situation worse; I

was always finding myself in the position of covering debts he had accumulated without my knowledge. Every time I wrote a check to pay a bill, I had a nagging fear that somehow Jose would have pulled the money out of the bank and the check would bounce.

His drinking and drug abuse continued to take an emotional toll on me and the never-ending drama that came with living with Jose was robbing me of any joy I might have had. In addition, I was a single mom, working at a low-paying job with no real prospects for improving my condition. And our child required special care, some of it very expensive.

If I had looked at the big picture in those days, I doubt I'd have been able to function. So I followed a simple philosophy: Focus on doing the best you can each day. Keep your head focused on what is most important and keep plugging.

My first priority, I realized, was getting back to work. I was working at MCM which is a collection agency at the time and it was about as steady of a job that I could get with no education, although there was nothing about the work that appealed to me in any sense. Working there did have one great advantage, however. The agency had its own daycare center next door and I was able to get Mycole a spot in the infant room. This meant I was able to check in on Mycole during breaks and at lunch, which – given his medical issues – was a blessing.

There were many days when I would get a call from the daycare center telling me that Mycole was having a seizure. Most of the time, the seizures stopped and he emerged no worse for the experience. But one day I got a call from the director, Beth (who later became one of Mycole's godmothers and a dear friend), Mycole was having a seizure, but this time he was spitting up blood. The paramedics were on the way, she told me.

In a state of panic, I rushed over to my boss, Chris, and told him what had happened and that I had to leave for the hospital.

He frowned.

"Your collection numbers have been low, you know," he said. "I think you really need to decide what is more important. If you don't have a job...."

I cut him off.

"I know what is more important," I said and left for the hospital.

After running a series of tests, doctors determined that Mycole was spitting up blood as a result of an allergy to his formula. He would need a special formula, I was told. It cost $25-$30 per can. I did the math in my head. How would I ever be able to pay for it? I was crushed.

From the start, I had enrolled in just about every government-sponsored program that was available for Mycole. With the intensive therapy Mycole's condition required, the costs were far more than I could manage. My finances were already shaky and my working relationship with my boss was damaged beyond repair. I was able to get a transfer to another team within the company, but found that in making the move my hourly wage went from $17.25 to $11.25.

I was heading in the wrong direction.

There was only one solution I could think of: I'd have to work a second job.

Under normal circumstances, I would not have minded working two jobs. But Mycole's condition made it all the more difficult. I was determined to provide him with the best care I could. That included giving him physical therapy at home to complement the P.T. he was receiving from Children Rehabilitative Services.

Somehow, I managed to do it all. I went back to work at Denny's. My shift at the collection agency went from 7 a.m. until 4 p.m. I worked the 5-10 p.m. shift at Denny's. On Saturdays, I would work the 2-10 p.m. shift, but I often worked a double-shift, which meant I started work at 2 p.m. Saturday and ended at 5 a.m. on Sunday.

Obviously, it was not the ideal situation. It seemed that I hardly had any time with Mycole. Because I was working two jobs, I had to take Mycole to a babysitter and, given my experience with Jose, I was always extremely anxious when I dropped Mycole off with a baby-sitter.

There were also reliability issues. Sometimes a baby-sitter would call and cancel at the last moment and I'd wind up hauling Mycole to Denny's with me. I would leave him in his car seat and set it up on the counter (in the non-smoking section) as I worked.

I was rushing back and forth between my customers and little Mycole one night when I realized that what I was doing was insane. I was physically exhausted, emotionally drained and desperately unhappy.

The next day I walked into the collection agency and quit on the spot. The working environment there, not to mention the nature of the work, was like poison to my soul. I had to get out.

Leaving the collection agency wasn't really all that great a risk. Jobs like that were a dime a dozen. The bigger problem was finding a career, something that would help me secure a real future for myself and Mycole.

On the way out of the collection agency, I went by the daycare and talked to Beth, who had become a supportive friend. I told her that I had quit the collection agency and I really didn't know what I was going to do next.

Beth had opened a charter school called Bright Ideas.

"Why don't you come at teach at my school?" she said. "I think you would be great with the kids."

I was very skeptical. First, I was a college drop-out and second, I had no teaching experience.

But Beth was not deterred. She still wanted to hire me. The job wouldn't pay well – only $7.50 per hour – but I could work in the school's daycare center after school. Also, Mycole would have free childcare for the entire day. He would be right next door to me all day. The more I thought about it, the better I liked the idea.

I went to work at Bright Ideas in the fall of 2000, teaching first, second and third grade classes and working in the daycare center before and after the school day had ended.

While I quickly fell in love with my students, I felt a little guilty. I knew that I was not really qualified to teach. Going back to school and being trained to teach seemed like the thing to do.

Although I was still working two jobs, waiting tables at Denny's I did not have to work on the weekend, which provided me with more time to spend with Mycole. When he was six months old, I enrolled him in a swimming class. I also started taking him to the library for story time. I would read and sing to him, give him physical therapy, pray for him and give him my full attention. Before long, I began to see results. His seizures came less and less frequently. Before he turned one year old, he had learned to crawl, to stand up and to walk. My son had recovered from his stroke; he was using his right hand as if nothing had ever happened. He was becoming a typical, active little boy.

With Mycole continuing to show improvement, I was able to focus a bit more of my attention on securing our future. I enrolled at Gateway Community College, going to classes at nights from Monday through Thursday. My friend, Patti, watched Mycole while I was at school.

I was in school, working toward a degree. Mycole was getting better every day.

But our finances, well, that was another story. Even though my apartment wasn't expensive, I realized that I couldn't afford the rent. I made the painful decision to apply for a spot in the city's subsidized housing (the projects) and moved into an apartment complex called Hill-N-Dale. Moving into the government housing made sense, financially, but it was a terrible environment to live in, especially for children. Drugs were everywhere. Shootings were common. Prostitutes were in and out of the complex at all hours. There were no playgrounds for the children. Some of the tenants seemed to have no regard for their living conditions or respect for the property. I hated going to the laundry room. More than once I found that someone had urinated into the washing machine. The trash cans were not changed frequently enough and seemed to be always overflowing.

I quickly began to refer to my new residence as "Hill-N-Hell." It was not much of an exaggeration. Mycole and I lived there for five years and I prayed for the day for us to leave. I consoled myself with the knowledge that living there was a necessary evil. I vowed to have a home of our own before Mycole finished kindergarten.

There wasn't much muscle behind that vow, I realized. I was still making less than $8 per hour and just beginning to get a college education.

The first tangible steps toward making that goal a reality came through a casual conversation with a friend. She mentioned that she was going through the qualification process for a Habitat for Humanity home. I had heard of the program, but knew none of the details.

She offered to take me with her the one of the Habitat meetings, so I could find out more about the program.

I was surprised to learn that there is a lot of work involved in qualifying. The Habitat program requires that would-be home owners take control of their finances and learn the skills necessary to be good homeowners.

I signed up for the program and immediately faced a hurdle: My credit. I was turned down on my initial attempt because I had outstanding debts on my credit report. I went to work trying to pay off my debts. But it seemed as though each time I got something cleared off my credit report, another old debt would emerge and I'd again be turned down by Habitat. Ultimately, I was turned down four times because of my credit. Finally, after four years of hard work to pay my past bills, it happened. My credit report came back clean. For the first time in 10 years, I was debt-free. I was accepted into the Habitat for Humanity program.

The work doesn't end there, though. Applicants are required to take classes on how to make a household budget. I was also required to put in 100 hours of work on another Habitat home as sweat equity.

Whatever the requirements were, I was determined to meet them.

I knew this was a real chance to escape the horrors of Hill-n-Dale. Finally, on July 15, 2005, we broke ground on my home. Mycole was there; and so were my whole family. During the next few months, Dad and Dwight, and Sharon helped with the construction, and Mom frequently watched Mycole.

There were some interesting parallels to my old life, I found. First, on the day we broke ground, the temperature was 115 degrees, the same temperature I had noticed on that thermometer the day I made my walk from the alley.

Second, my home was built in downtown Phoenix in an area they called – you guessed it – The Zone. Part of Habitat's strategy is to rehabilitate neighborhoods by building new homes. Habitat believes that there is something profoundly important about home ownership. The pride of being a stakeholder can transform neighborhoods.

All the while, I was going to school at night, teaching in the day and sometimes working at Denny's on Saturdays. Somehow, I found time to be involved in homeless ministries and singing at my church.

As the day of our move approached, I was wrapping up my undergraduate work. I had transferred from Gateway Community College to the University of Phoenix, where I would earn my degree in Human Services.

I had reached two major milestones at once, it seemed.

I was a college graduate. And I was a homeowner.

For the first time in a long time, the future seemed hopeful.

But I wasn't finished, I told myself.

"This is just the beginning."

Chapter 14
"Finding My Shoes"

On a late October day in 2005, I packed up my belongings, loaded them in a U-Haul truck and left Hill-n-Dale for my new home.

Although no one would mistake my new neighborhood for paradise, I welcomed the changes it represented. Mycole and I had a home of our own and Mycole had a yard to play in. There weren't many children on our street; the few that did live nearby spoke only Spanish. But Mycole did have his friends from school and I looked forward to having his friends over to play now that we were settled in a home.

The Much Love name had been bought by someone else, so I changed the name of my ministry to Finding My Shoes. We partnered up with St. Vincent de Paul and Phoenix Rescue Mission. What we were doing was not much different from the ministry's previous incarnation, except that instead of holding our monthly rallies outside, we held them inside buildings so that people could shower, change clothes, get a hot meal, a haircut, a backpack, and of course, new socks and shoes.

I was grateful for all the blessings I had received and well aware of how far I had already come. But I knew that Mycole and I weren't yet at the end of our journey. One evening I sat at the kitchen table and began to think about what I wanted to do with my life. Although financial freedom and the security that

comes with it were important, I began to sense that there was a greater purpose out there on the horizon.

During my desperate days on the streets, I remember how getting off crack and off the streets had been a cherished dream. But once I had been freed from addiction, the same streets kept calling me back. For years, I had returned to the streets trying to offer love, support and encouragement to the people with whom I had once shared a lifestyle.

Somehow, I felt I could do more.

I knew that I could relate to these people in a special way. Many can offer sympathy; I could offer empathy. I knew these people. I knew the despair of addiction, the self-loathing, the fear, the hopelessness.

I also knew that I had beaten the odds that seemed so heavily stacked against me. If I could break the chains of addiction, homelessness and violence that kept me bound to the streets, others could do it, too. Through my experiences, I could help others.

In order to achieve that goal, I realized that I needed the best education available. I decided to get a PhD.

I laughed at myself. "Dr. Brenda Combs. Wouldn't that be something?"

I went on-line and started looking for graduate programs that were similar to the University of Phoenix, which is where I got my college degree. I was looking for programs that offered flexible class schedules, since I knew that I'd be working full-time.

Three schools seemed to fit my needs: The University of Phoenix, North Central University and Grand Canyon University.

I called all three schools and spoke with enrollment counselors. The counselor I spoke with at Grand Canyon really made a connection with me that clinched my decision to attend

GCU. Her name was Stephanie Sweeting and she was not only a counselor, but a student herself in the Master's program at GCU.

I explained to her that I was working two jobs, so the class schedules were going to be a challenge.

"Why don't you enroll in our online Master's program?" she asked.

I was skeptical, at first. I didn't have access to a reliable computer, for one thing. Second, I didn't really know if I had the discipline necessary to succeed in an online program.

Stephanie reassured me.

"Hey, I'm the same program," she said enthusiastically. "We can do it together. I'll help."

I didn't know it at the time, but Grand Canyon University was going through an amazing transition.

A low-key local businessman named Brent Richardson invested in this small, failing, nondenominational Christian university.

Richardson, an entrepreneur who had succeeded in developing educational enterprises, had a vision for a new kind of university, one that would combine the strengths of a traditional university with the strengths of the emerging online university concept.

Of course, I didn't know any of that when I enrolled at GCU. All I knew was that the school seemed genuinely interested in helping me achieve my dreams. I even got a scholarship to help defray the costs.

I began my graduate studies at Grand Canyon University on Jan. 5, 2006. That first day of class was a mixture of excitement and anxiety as I sat in front of my computer and logged into the GCU website. When I saw the syllabus, I was terrified.

I said a little prayer, asking God to open my mind to the information I was going to be receiving.

And then I went to work.

It wasn't easy, of course. There were many nights when I would return home after working two jobs and getting Mycole off to bed that I would sit down at the computer and work on my assignments into the early-morning hours. There were also times when my old computer simply refused to cooperate and I'd find myself scrambling to find time to go to the library to do my class work on the computers there.

I made it through my first eight-week class, though, and that gave me confidence. "I can do this!" I remember saying.

I also realized that I was not taking full advantage of the greatest asset of an online program: School was in session 24/7. Originally, I had prepared myself to spend three years in the Master's program. I wondered if I could shorten that time-frame.

"Sure," Stephanie told me. "Just double up on your classes."

"Sign me up," I said, taking a deep breath, fully aware of the load I would soon be carrying.

But there was something about GCU's program that seemed to carry me forward. It was difficult, but at every turn I always seemed to get the support and encouragement I needed to keep pressing on.

I didn't know it at the time, but other people were beginning to take notice. By this time Bright Ideas Charter School had closed its doors and I was running the summer program and teaching second and third grade at StarShine Academy. My students and the staff were my biggest fans. I shared my life story with the students and staff to encourage them to believe in themselves and never let go of their dreams. My students sent letters to Oprah Winfrey, suggesting that I would be a good guest to have on her show.

Without my knowledge I was nominated for a teaching award. Just as I was finishing up my Masters studies, I was notified that I had been included in "Who's Who Among American's Teachers."

Suddenly, my story began to circulate.

A local TV reporter came and did a story on my unique journey. Then, Faith Weese, GCU's Chief of University Relations, and Bill Jenkins, GCU's Public Relations Director, stepped in. Bill took the letters my students had written and mailed them to the producers of the Oprah Winfrey Show. Faith met with me to talk about a special award I was going to receive during commencement ceremonies.

The day of the commencement ceremonies seemed almost dream-like. I was picked up a big white limousine and taken to a VIP Luncheon before the ceremonies, which I thought would certainly be the highlight of the day. I figured that was my moment in the sun, and I was thrilled to have it.

I told Faith how much I appreciated everything. She just laughed.

"You're in for a few more surprises yet," she said, smiling.

Bill had arranged for a bus to pick up my students at StarShine and bring them to the commencement ceremony. Meanwhile, I was stunned to hear that a TV crew was on hand to do a story.

As all of the students lined up to begin the march into the stadium, the music began to play and I found it hard to keep my emotions in check. I began to reflect on this long, hard journey. I thought of my days of living as a crack addict, homeless and filthy and hopeless. I thought of how hard I had worked to escape that miserable existence. I thought of the times when Mycole was sick and I didn't know what to do. I thought of the long nights of studying, of the times when I had to go to the library to work because my computer had broken down. I thought of 10 years of working two or three jobs just to make ends meet.

When we entered the stadium, I scanned to crowd, looking for Mycole. Then something else caught my eye as I was filing past the VIP section: My students! They saw me and went wild, yelling out my name, holding up signs they had made for me.

It was all I could do to keep from collapsing in tears of joy.

Finally, we reached our seats. A student next to me looked at me.

"Where's your speech?" she asked.

"Huh?" I said. "What speech? I don't know what you're talking about."

She just laughed.

After the keynote speech, an image was flashed up on the big screen.

It was my picture.

And suddenly, there was a video of me from the story that had appeared on the local TV broadcasts. At the end of the video, a voice boomed out over the loudspeakers: "Miss Brenda Combs."

Somehow, I managed to get to my feet and float across the stage where I was presented with the Distinguished Teacher Award.

As I was about to return to my seat, Faith caught me by my elbow.

"We have a message for you from a very special lady who has heard your story," she said.

Suddenly, music was playing and a large image was projected onto the big screen – First Lady Laura Bush.

Faith read her message and it was all I could do to keep from falling out from the shock of it all.

I'll never forget that night. And to be honest, there are times when I still feel like so much of what was to follow is more a dream than reality.

A week later I appeared on CNN. I was joined on the set by Brent Richardson as I told my story to CNN host Rick Sanchez. At the end of the interview, Sanchez asked me what I intended to do next.

I told him that I wanted to pursue a doctorate degree. Sanchez noted that getting a doctorate would probably cost a lot of money. He asked if I had that kind of money.

"No, but I'll figure it out somehow," I said.

Sanchez then turned his attention to Brent.

"What do think?" he said. "Can you help her out?"

I was floored by the question.

"I think so," Brent said, as he picked up what looked to me like a diploma. "This is a full-ride scholarship at Grand Canyon University," he said. "We want you to be our first candidate in our first online doctorate program."

I was too stunned to speak. I could feel the tears welling up in my eyes.

Could this be true? It was. I had a full-ride scholarship. But that wasn't all. I was interviewed by *Reader's Digest* who published an article about me titled "Class Act" in the November 2007 issue.

With the publicity my story received, I soon began to field calls from all over the country from groups wanting me to share my story. In the months that followed, I found myself sitting at the NBC Studios in New York, making an appearance on The Today Show.

One day, as I was visiting Faith on the GCU campus, and I ran into Richardson.

He wanted to know how things were going. He wanted to know about my plans for the future.

I told him that I wanted to make the most of the opportunities I had to travel and tell my story. I wanted to be able to have a great career that would allow me to stop working two or three jobs to make ends meet. I wanted to be able to give Mycole more of my time and attention. I wanted to be able to take Mycole to school when started and pick him up when school gets out; versus taking him to daycare in the morning, sending him to the after school program and then picking him up from there and taking him with me to my other job.

Richardson listened to me intently. I also told him that I wanted to take Mycole on "real life" field trips, because Mycole will learn more visiting the White House than he ever would just reading about it in a book.

A few days later, he named me as the Ambassador of Inspiration and Achievement for Grand Canyon University.

And once again my world changed. My heart overflows with gratitude.

I went home that day, hit my knees in my living room, and began to sob uncontrollably. Everything I had asked God to grant me had been given to me. I wasn't a drug addict. I wasn't homeless. I had a beautiful, healthy child. I had an education. Now, I had a job sharing my story and inspiring others to believe in themselves and make their dreams come true.

That day in my living room, as I thanked God and wept, a new thought came to me.

I thought of that day when my shoes were stolen off my feet, of how I had walked through an alley on bleeding, blistered feet toward a destiny I could never have imagined.

My struggle was over, I thought, but my journey has just begun.

I have found my shoes.

Epilogue

*"I crashed down and I tumbled, but I did not crumble, I was
not built to break. I didn't know my own strength."*
~~*Whitney Houston*

When you are on the streets, people – even the people you
are closest to - tend to drift in and out of your life. Some go to
prison. Some go to the cemetery. Some just disappear and you
never know what became of them.

Although it's been more than a dozen years since I was
mercifully delivered from life on the streets, I still find myself
drawn to those old familiar haunts – The Zone, the 7th Ave.
Bridge, Interfaith and C.A.S.S. and "Vinny's."

I go there not so much to remind myself of how far I've come,
but to reach out to those who are still suffering from the results
of drug addiction and homelessness.

Whenever I see some of my old friends from my days on the
street, there are conflicting emotions: I am happy to know that
they are still alive. I am sad to know that they are still bound to
such a cruel, soul-starving lifestyle.

There are other friends that I don't see. My hope is that they
have a story similar to mine; that they have beat the odds and
escaped the streets. I know, though, that many have met a far
more tragic end.

Tony, my "Mob & Rob" partner, disappeared before that
fateful day when I walked out of the alley and into a new life. I
wouldn't know what happened to him until one day when I was
visiting the Zone as part of a homeless ministry function.

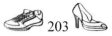

He had been convicted on drug charges and sent to prison for five years. During his five years in prison, Tony worked on beating his addiction. Each day, he told himself that, no matter what might happen, he was going to live a sober life when he got out of prison. He was determined to put his life in order.

On the day he was released, he took the bus ride from the prison to Phoenix. An hour after stepping off the bus, Tony got high.

One day as I was handing out bottled waters in Jurassic Park, Glen called me and told me that Tony was there in the Zone getting high.

"My Tony?" I asked.

"Yes, your Tony."

A few minutes later, I came upon Tony, lying on the ground by Interfaith. One look and I knew he had been smoking crack.

Tony looked up at me.

I paused for a moment. I couldn't speak. It broke my heart to see him in that condition. I drove away without a word being exchanged. Although I continued to visit the Zone as part of various community service events, I never saw Tony there again.

But a few years later, as I entered a classroom at University of Phoenix, I heard a voice calling my name. I turned. There was Tony, smiling. He looked good, fit and – most surprising of all – genuinely happy.

After class, we sat and talked. Tony had been sober from the moment he saw me that day at the park, he said.

"I can't really explain it," he told me. "But when I saw the expression on your face, the hurt in your eyes, it did something to me. It was almost like someone was holding up a mirror and I was seeing myself for the first time. I hated what I saw. And that was when I knew that I had to change or die."

It wasn't easy. If you are an addict, you might as well get used to the idea: It's never easy.

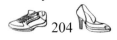

But Tony made it.

Tony and I got married December 2009. While I don't know where our journey will take us, I do know that two hopeless, homeless drug addicts have been given a great gift.

It is a gift too precious to waste. I guess that's the whole point of this book.

Novelist Tom Robbins wrote that "it's never too late to have a happy childhood." I would amend that by saying that it's never too late to have a happy life.

No two journeys are alike, I realize, but all journeys can reach the same destination – a life filled with purpose, meaning and joy.

If I can do it, you can do it, too.

And this is my prayer for you:

Hope when things seem most hopeless. Believe when you feel all faith is gone. Press on through the pain. Don't stop. Keep walking until you find your shoes.

For Booking/Speaking request

Please contact:
Laura Schultz Holden
The Butler Lappert Williams Firm
250 Park Avenue
7th Floor
New York, NY 10177

(212)572-4842 Office
(212)658-9500 Fax

lh@blwfirm.com
www.blwfirm.com

Follow Dr. Brenda Combs on social media

www.brendacombs.com

www.findingmyshoes.com

www.facebook.com/pages/Brenda-Combs/164952615168

www.twitter.com/brendarcombs

www.instagram.com/brendacombs

About The Author

Dr. Brenda Combs travels the country sharing her story with schools, churches, workshops, and conferences inspiring others to believe that they can make their dreams become reality. Brenda is a strong supporter of higher education and the fight to end homelessness and is a nationally recognized and respected motivational speaker, and respected educator, and inspiring actress. Dr. Combs lives in Phoenix, Arizona with her husband Tony, her son Mycole, and Pops.